THEY CALLED ME GOD

THE BEST UMPIRE WHO EVER LIVED

DOUG HARVEY

AND **PETER GOLENBOCK**

G

GALLERY BOOKS

NEW YORK LONDON TORONTO SYDNEY NEW DELHI

G
Gallery Books
A Division of Simon & Schuster, Inc.
1230 Avenue of the Americas
New York, NY 10020

First Gallery Books hardcover edition March 2014

Interior design by Jaime Putorti
Jacket design by Jason Gabbert Design LLC
Jacket photograph from the Doug Harvey Collection

Manufactured in the United States of America

10 9 8 7 6 5 4 3 2 1

Library of Congress Control Number: 2013048063

ISBN 978-1-4767-4878-8
ISBN 978-1-4767-4881-8 (ebook)

To my wife, Joy,

who made it all possible

CONTENTS

THEY CALLED ME GOD

CHAPTER 1

A WONDERFUL LIFE

— 1 —

I've had a wonderful life. I was an umpire in the major leagues for thirty-one years, from 1962, when John F. Kennedy was president, until 1992, the end of the George H. W. Bush presidency. That's a lot of games: 4,673, to be exact. During that time I don't believe I ever made a wrong call. Perhaps that's why the players lovingly referred to me as God.

The Society for American Baseball Research voted me the second-best umpire in the last hundred and something years, taking a backseat only to Bill Klem, who was known by his admirers as the Old Arbitrator and by his detractors as Catfish, because they said he looked like one.

When they called to tell me that I had finished second only

to Mr. Klem, rather than acting pleased, I told them I was offended.

"Dig him up," I told them. "Let's have a go at it." I said that because I like to think I don't take second place to anybody. If they brought back Bill Klem, I'd be happy to go head-to-head with him anytime. Have a little contest.

There's an old saying that they hire you to be the best, and then they expect you to be even better. For me, that's what umpiring is all about. It's a tough racket, believe me.

Often I'm asked to give young umpires advice, and here's my most important piece of advice: When you're umpiring behind the plate, stop trying to be perfect right now, because if you're that hard on yourself, you're not going to make it. You'll have a nervous breakdown before you get out of high school ball. There was just one perfect umpire, and they put him on the cross. At the end of the day, the hardest part of the job of umpiring behind the plate is not beating yourself up when the game is over. I've seen guys—professionals—walk around in a panic for three days straight because they know on the fourth day they'll be behind the plate again. Umpiring behind the plate is, after all, the hardest part of the game.

I can tell you this because I was as guilty of doing this as anyone. Every day I knocked myself out, trying to be as perfect as possible. When a pitcher wound up, I would watch him, and it was just me and the ball. Watching that pitch—watching every pitch—would take so much out of me. When I strode onto the field, the outside world would disappear, especially that last month of the season when it really tore at your guts. You didn't want to miss a thing. During games toward the end of the season I had a feeling of being mesmerized.

I gave it everything I had, and when I stepped off the airplane coming home at the end of the season, my wife, Joy, said I looked like walking death. I'd be completely worn out.

I am very proud of my profession. Without the umpires, the game wouldn't survive. I can remember during one of my early years in Major League Baseball I umpired a spring-training game in Arizona between the San Diego Padres and the Cleveland Indians. After the game was over, one of the managers came to me and asked if my crew and I would stay and umpire three more innings. This took place in the early 1960s, when major league umpires were barely making a living wage. I didn't think it right that we should be asked to work overtime for nothing, and so I told them we'd do it for $25 each. It wasn't like I was asking for the moon.

"Screw it," the manager told me. "We don't need you. The catcher for each team can do it just as easily."

This was the sort of disrespect we were used to back then. Our crew walked toward the backstop, and as we were starting to walk off the field, a riot broke out. Twenty players were in a stack. It hadn't taken ten minutes.

The Padres' catcher was calling balls and strikes, and he called a pitch a strike, and the Cleveland batter said, "Are you shitting me?"

"No," said the catcher, who stood up and took off his mask,

and the batter slugged him. Before I knew it, both teams were mixing it up on the field. All because there were no umpires. Baseball, you see, isn't a game you play on the honor system.

The umpire is there for one reason and one reason only: to make sure one team doesn't gain an unfair advantage. In tougher words, to make sure one side doesn't cheat. It's that simple. For the game to have meaning, it has to be fair. The only thing standing between fairness and chaos is the umpiring crew.

— 2 —

Throughout my entire career, my emphasis was on integrity. I never wanted to be accused of bias, and I never wanted to be charged with giving anything less than my best, no matter whether it was the first week of the season or the last, whether the two teams were fighting for a pennant or whether the game had no meaning in the standings.

It was the last week of the 1975 season, and I was umpiring a series in which the first-place Cincinnati Reds were playing the last-place Houston Astros. The Reds had clinched it, and Sparky Anderson, the manager, announced he was going to play his second-stringers.

I was the crew chief and I was umpiring on the bases that day. I called my crew together. I wanted to make sure none of the other guys decided to make calls with the purpose of speeding up the game and getting us back to the hotel.

"Hey, fellas," I said. "You may have a guy on the bad club, if he bats .240 he gets twice the raise. You have no right to mess with that. Just call the game the way it is."

I didn't want to do what I had seen other crews do: Just call strikes in order to get this meaningless game over as fast as they could. I could see who was in a hurry and who wasn't, who had a good strike zone and who didn't. And so could the players.

To be an umpire you have to be willing to sacrifice, and those sacrifices can be physical as well as mental. In my first year umpiring, St. Louis Cardinals pitcher Bob Gibson threw a pitch and the catcher missed it, and the ball caromed under my mask and broke off two teeth, which I spit onto the ground.

Fellow umpire Shag Crawford came over.

"You're bleeding," he said. "You should have someone look at it. Let's get you out of the game."

My pride was in my work. For me to leave the field they would've had to carry me off. I wouldn't do that to my partners. They would have to work one man short if I left.

"Hold it, Shag," I said. "It doesn't make any difference whether I'm sitting in a waiting room at the hospital or umpiring baseball. I'd prefer umpiring baseball."

I told him I would attend to it after the game.

The next day a dentist told me I would need to take time off for him to work on my damaged mouth, but I said no. He gave me a shot to stop the bleeding, and I went on to umpire that afternoon.

The bleeding continued off and on, and I used chewing tobacco to stanch it during the last few weeks of the season. I was in misery.

I went to another dentist, who packed my mouth with cotton, but still the bleeding continued.

Two months later my mouth was infected.

Before that, I was in Pittsburgh umpiring the Game of the Week: the Pirates against the San Francisco Giants. All the way across the country, my wife, Joy, was at home in California giving birth to our first child. At the time, commissioner Ford Frick didn't allow us to go home for the birth of a child. After the game, I got a call. Joy had given birth to a son, whom we named Scott.

I didn't get to see him until he was two weeks old.

That's what I call sacrifice.

That's some of what I gave up for my profession.

— 3 —

In all of baseball history there are only ten umpires in the National Baseball Hall of Fame, and I'm proud to say that I'm one of them. I was elected in 2010. The other umpires who were elected are Jocko Conlan, my former crew chief; Al Barlick, another of my former crew chiefs; Hank O'Day, who umped in the nineteenth century; Tommy Connolly, who was active from 1901 until 1931; Bill Klem, who was an umpire from 1905 to 1941; Bill McGowan,

Cal Hubbard, Billy Evans, and Nestor Chylak, who were all in the game for between twenty and thirty years. All were cited for their character and their umpiring skill. Being elected to the Hall is an honor I will always cherish until the day I die—which, by the way, may occur sooner rather than later. I have been stricken with cancer, and the diagnosis isn't great.

"What's my chance of living through this?" I asked my doctor.

"Well, not that good," he said.

"What are my chances?"

"Fifty percent," he said.

"I'll beat that," I told him. "You want to know why? Because every day I walked out onto that field with three other fine gentlemen, and nobody in the stands of sixty thousand people liked us when a call went against their team. Moreover, two ball clubs didn't give a shit whether we lived or died. Fighting cancer is a lot easier. I know I can beat this."

If you're going to live, attitude is everything. And that's the way it was with my work. I loved my job. I hated when we had a day off. I didn't know what to do with myself. I couldn't wait to get back on the field. If I had a two-week vacation, I couldn't wait to go back behind the plate my first day back. Everyone else wanted to get their feet wet, to start at third base and work their way around to second and then to first before going back behind the plate. The fewest calls during a ball game are made at third base.

Not me. I wanted to make sure I could still umpire balls and strikes.

During one off-season I went to Baja California looking for an engine for my Model A. I stepped out of my car to ask where the guy who owned the engine lived, and a German shepherd came out of nowhere and tore up my left leg. I had to get twenty-two stitches.

In the hospital, they put a white salve on the wound and wrapped me in wet sheets and put ice over it. I laid like that for hours.

Fred Fleig, the National League secretary-treasurer in charge of the league's umpires, called me in the hospital.

"Doug," he said, "why don't you stay home for spring training and get your energy back?"

"Fred," I said, "why don't I get my ass back to spring training and see if I can still umpire?" That's the way I was.

The doctor ordered me to take time off. But to my mind there was no place for time off. You have to get back to what you know and love.

I'm sharing this so those youngsters who desire to become umpires—or just baseball fans in general who appreciate the intricacies of the game—can understand how I did what I did for as long as I did. I also want them to appreciate how blessed I've been to have been allowed to work on the hallowed baseball diamonds across America for so many years.

I firmly believe that Babe Ruth had it right. When Ruth was dying, baseball honored him by giving him a day, and in his speech at Yankee Stadium he remarked, "The only real game in the world, I think, is baseball. You've got to start way down at the bottom, when you're six or seven, and if you're successful and you try hard enough, you're bound to come out on top."

The Babe could have been talking about me. I knew I wanted to be an umpire when I was six years old. My dad was an umpire—and a damn fine one—and I wanted to be just like him. I wanted nothing more than to be out on that field, and I umpired in the major leagues for thirty-one wonderful years, and for that I'm very grateful.

I loved what I did, loved the feeling of camaraderie, the feeling of togetherness, the feeling that, *Hey, we are who we are: We're umpires.*

Here's just a little bit of what I learned and experienced along the way. I wish I could still be out there. I never should have retired. I've regretted it ever since. I'm telling you, baseball today could still use Doug Harvey.

CHAPTER 2

A NOT-SO-EASY CHILDHOOD

— 1 —

I came along on March 13, 1930, at the beginning of the Depression. When I was growing up my parents didn't have much, but they gave me lots of love, a strong work ethic, and a strong sense of integrity.

Until I was ten, we lived in South Gate, a suburb of Los Angeles, and every week Dad would bring home a big sack of beans and one of flour, and my mom would make gravy from the flour and she'd cook the beans. Those were our staples. For meat once a week, Dad would get off work, get in his old car, and take a .22-caliber rifle up to Chavez Ravine. It was a large, empty field then, but today it's the site of Dodger Stadium. He'd take me or one of my older brothers with him every once in a while, and he'd prowl the area, hunting rabbit or quail. Dad was one of the greatest shots I ever saw. It was how we got our meat. He was making $28 a month, and Mom was a waitress and later a cashier for a Safeway supermarket, and with that small amount of money they had to pay for rent, utilities, food, and clothes for four kids. Times were tough.

My mother, who was born in Oklahoma in 1906, was one of eleven children. She was a full-blooded American Indian, a mix of Cherokee and Choctaw. My grandparents lived in the Indian Territories, where they were cared for and fed by the federal government. It was a precarious existence. They weren't allowed to work, because back then an Indian was not permitted to take a white man's job. Making life even more difficult, my grandparents had intermarried—a Cherokee marrying a Choctaw—so neither was accepted by the other's tribe. Six weeks after my mother was born, my grandparents decided life in California would be better. My mom's much older brother was living in Los Angeles, and my mom's parents moved there to get away from a bare existence and to be near him. They moved to the suburb of Blythe, south and east of downtown L.A.

My dad was twenty-five years old when he married Mom. I have no idea how they met. I once saw a picture of Mom when she was in her twenties. She was a gorgeous, raven-haired beauty.

My parents had a good relationship, marred only by my dad's occasional wandering eye. Dad was a playboy type, and he'd chase the broads a little bit. My mother never forgave him for it, but she bit her tongue and lived with it.

They had four children. My oldest brother was named Royal Demoss Harvey. He was called Roy. Next came Nolan Devoin Harvey. His middle name—Devoin—came from a French lady who watched us, because both Dad and Mom worked.

When I was born, I was named Harold Douglas Harvey.

— 2 —

My dad's name was Harold Harvey, and every time my mom would holler "Harold," both of us would come running.

When I was about six Dad finally said, "Enough of that. From now on, your name is Doug," and that's why everyone calls me that.

My younger brother was named Donald Ray, but we called him Donnie.

When I was four years old, I developed nephritis, a kidney infection that killed the movie actress Jean Harlow a few years later. I too was supposed to die, but I'm alive because my parents refused to accept defeat.

The infection was bad. My belly looked like I had swallowed a watermelon. A doctor in the Queen of Angels Hospital in Los Angeles told my parents, "Take him home. There's no chance of him surviving. He'll be dead in six weeks."

My parents, refusing to give up on their child, instead took me to the Children's Hospital in L.A., where the first woman surgeon in California history treated me by cutting me open, pulling my insides out and cleaning them, and then stuffing them back into my body. When I tell doctors that, they tell me, "That's insane. Nobody in the world would do a thing like that," but that's what she did, and I have two huge scars running across my belly to prove it.

I spent my fifth and sixth birthdays at home recovering, a total of twenty-two months that I spent in bed. As you can imagine, I spent a lot of time by myself those two years. Since we didn't have a TV or radio back then, for entertainment I had to satisfy myself with some pretty simple things.

A nurse would come to see me three times a day to give me an oily substance to keep my bowels moving. She'd take a tongue depressor, dip it in this cod liver oil, and give it to me to suck on.

I was so sick I was limited to drinking one teaspoon of water each hour. Oh, I was dying of thirst. My dad, who worked as an iceman for the Union Ice Company, said to the doctors, "Wait a minute. If he can have moisture but he can't have it in liquid form, I wonder whether he can suck on ice?"

He brought in a bucket of ice and chipped it up, and the nurses would feed me little pieces of it. It was a method that eventually was used everywhere for patients who had what I had. Many years later, the ice was changed to watermelon.

I was in the hospital in 1935 and 1936, an age when airplanes were in the news and very popular with us kids. The nurse would take two tongue depressors and attach them together with a rubber band so the two sticks would look like an airplane, and she would give it to me to play with. I would spend hours pretending I was a pilot flying my plane around as I recovered.

That's how I started life: by beating death.

After I was released by the hospital and returned home, on Sundays I would sit on our back porch and watch real airplanes fly to and from the Los Angeles National Airport. I would spend my Sundays eating fruit and watching this one airplane climb higher and higher, going around in circles, and then the plane would straighten out, and I could see a passenger jump out of the plane and parachute down.

As soon as I saw him, I would holler, "There he is! There he is!"

I don't know whether he was getting paid to do that or whether he was doing it for fun, but every Sunday I would watch him, and he became part of my Sunday entertainment.

When I got out of the hospital, I put my two feet on the floor and immediately collapsed. My legs were too weak to support my body. There was no way I could walk.

When I got home, I was determined to walk again. I was the type of person who would set his mind to something and then do it. It took me awhile to build up the strength in my legs, but it wasn't too long before I was walking again.

— 3 —

My father, Harold, was my idol. He taught me the meaning of hard work. He also taught me the importance of honesty and fairness. For eighteen years he worked for the Union Ice Company. He'd report for work at four thirty in the morning and work all day. His job was to cut up three-hundred-pound blocks of ice and put them in hundred-pound sacks. He then would deliver those hundred-pound sacks to all the bars in downtown Los Angeles.

Dad was a strong man, and I was with him on the day that his fellow workers bet him he couldn't carry one of those three-hundred-pound blocks of ice across Figueroa Boulevard, which was a wide, heavily trafficked major thoroughfare in L.A. It was 1937, and he bet his entire paycheck—$28—that he could do it. His coworkers made smaller bets—of $1 to $5—that he couldn't.

Dad weighed about 180 pounds. I watched as he hoisted the huge block of ice on his broad shoulders while his coworkers went out into the street and stopped the traffic. Somehow he carried the block of ice all the way across six lanes of traffic to win the bet.

He then turned and began heading back the other way.

"You can put it down now," yelled a coworker. "Our bet was only one way."

Ignoring him, my dad carried the bulky block of ice back across the boulevard.

"You damn fool," said another coworker. "All you had to do was take it across one way. Why did you do that?"

"Because it's not my ice," he said. "It doesn't belong to me."

You see, my dad had integrity.

He also had pride.

The ice company was a family business, and the head of the company told Dad that if he died, Dad was going to take it over and run it. When the owner died in 1940, he instead left the company to a son who had never actually worked for the Union Ice Company. The son came in and insisted he was going to run it. You had to know my dad. He had one standard: Something was fair, or it was unfair.

He taught me so much in the way of fairness, and this is what I brought with me to the game of baseball.

After working for the ice company for eighteen years, my dad said, "The hell with you," and he quit.

I was ten years old.

— 4 —

My dad then got a job 150 miles south of Los Angeles, not far from San Diego in the Imperial Valley, working as a truck driver, hauling cantaloupes from the fields to the packing shed. I don't know exactly how it came about, except that my dad was a truck driver, and this was another truck-driving job. It was steady work.

Dad knew the owner of the company, and maybe he mentioned he was bringing his family down, so the guy said, "I have a house for you to live in if you take care of the property."

The house was on a pig ranch. The company owner needed someone to feed the pigs and milk his cows.

I thought my dad had sold us to hell.

I mean it.

My father had moved there first, and so my brother Roy, who was only fourteen, drove Mom, Nolan, and me from L.A. to the small town of El Centro. We arrived there about midnight. It was 92 degrees, usual for summer in the desert of the Imperial Valley, and I was miserable. When I stepped out of the car my shoes made a crunching sound. The ground was covered with a sea of crickets. You couldn't walk without stepping on one.

El Centro, I soon learned, was located in the Mojave Desert of Southern California. Temperatures reached as high as 125 degrees in the summer. To put it mildly, it took some getting used to.

Dad would dump a large load of cantaloupes in our driveway, and one of my jobs when I was in grade school was to feed the cantaloupes to the pigs. We also had eight cows, and it was my brother Roy's job to milk them.

At first I hated that we had to leave L.A., but it turned out to be the best thing that happened to us. L.A.'s smog was bad, and when my brothers were freshmen at Garfield High School they were threatened by the pachucos, the Latino hoods who roamed the school. Around the same time the engineers who drove the L.A. streetcars went on strike, and I can remember my dad telling me of the time the strikers were rocking his streetcar and he had to punch a couple of them so the people on the car could get off before they were injured.

Still, I can't believe Dad moved us to El Centro. It was in the middle of nowhere, but it was agricultural country, a place where the people had a strong work ethic, so we fit right in.

We often went to the Imperial fairgrounds and watched the cowboys rope, ride, and steer-wrestle. When I was in high school I went over to a friend's house, and we were looking for something to do. It was hot inside the house. There was no air-conditioning, only a fan to keep us cool. I looked out the window and saw some kind of contraption in the backyard, and I asked him what it was.

"Let me show you," he said, and he took a rope and lassoed a calf, and put him in the chute. He went and got his horse, put on a saddle, and hopped on.

"Turn him loose," he yelled, and when I pulled a rope, the calf went running out. My friend rode after him, jumped on top of the calf, and wrestled it to the ground.

"Want to try it?" he asked.

"No thanks," I said. I had no desire to become a cowboy.

We went to motorcycle races and watched the midget racers go at each other. I drove go-karts a few times, but I never raced them. Go-karts were first invented in the Imperial Valley. The first ones had engines taken from washing machines, which in the 1940s were powered by gasoline. I never had an interest in cars like some of my friends.

— 5 —

What I did was play sports year-round. When I got to high school I played football, and at the end of the season turned in my football gear and drew my basketball gear. Then I'd turn that in and get my baseball gear. In the summer you would try to find a job part-time, and you played softball in the evenings. On Sundays you played baseball. That was the life.

When I entered Central Union High School (now El Centro High School) in the ninth grade I didn't weigh a hundred pounds. I didn't want to play football. I didn't particularly like getting tackled, but my brothers Roy and Nolan had gone there, and they had played and done well. When the school secretary learned I was their brother, she took me to the football coach, who took me right into the gym and issued me a football uniform. I played three years of varsity football.

As a kid, I didn't root for any particular team or have a favorite player. Isn't that funny I didn't have a team? I was always neutral, even as a kid.

— 6 —

It was a decent life growing up in El Centro, and if I had thought about it, I would have taken my children there to raise them. People laugh about my being out in the country, hot as it was, but I learned a lot growing up there.

Most of all, what I learned was common sense. I learned that if you stuck your hand where it didn't belong—say, in the motor of one of those midget racers—you could get your hand cut off. If you walked in the wrong place where a herd of cattle were grazing, you might get run over by a stampede.

They don't teach common sense in the city. In the city they taught you who could be the toughest. My common sense is what I brought to umpiring. It's what gave me a leg up on other umpires.

The year after we moved to El Centro, the war broke out when the Japanese attacked Pearl Harbor on December 7, 1941. My dad became the civilian personnel director at the army base of Camp Lockett in Campo, east of San Diego and just north of the Mexican border. He was making good money. The base housed the last cavalry units in the U.S. Army. I'm perhaps the last person ever to have seen a cavalry charge. The men and their horses would go out into the mountains, and they'd be gone for a week. They gathered on a Saturday near where I lived, and on Sunday we would sit on our front porch. From there we'd see the horses line up at one end of a long field; we could hear the bugle sounding the charge, and here they would come in full charge, galloping across the field.

As the war pressed on, the army replaced the cavalry with armored vehicles, tanks, and half-tracks. I was sorry not to be able to watch those cavalry charges anymore.

— 7 —

As civilian director of the base, my father could leave anytime he wanted. When we moved to Imperial Valley, my dad started umpiring. My dad had played third base for the Union Ice Company baseball team. Our family would go out to the ballpark every weekend, and I would sit and watch his games. Back then you could do that without worrying about a child being stolen. He had been an umpire in Los Angeles, and when he arrived in El Centro he introduced himself around and became one of the most highly respected umpires in the region. As long as things were running smoothly, the commandant let Dad go on a Friday night to umpire a high school game. Heck, the commander probably had a kid playing on the team.

Dad was the best umpire I ever saw. He was very fair: He had four sons who played ball at El Centro High School, and yet for the twelve years we were in school the opposing coaches knew that our being on the team made no difference to my dad.

They always asked, "Can Mr. Harvey call balls and strikes?" even though they knew his sons were playing on the home team. That's how fair my father was.

After the war Dad got a job selling tickets for the El Centro Imperials, a Class A professional team in the Sunset League. Dad also was the stand-in umpire in case one of the umpires hired by the league got sick or couldn't make a game. Emmett Ashford, the first African American umpire in the major leagues, got his start working the Sunset League. Emmett worked with my dad, and a couple of times my dad invited him over to the house for a beer.

When I was sixteen years old I began umpiring semipro and industrial-league softball and baseball games. I was able to do that because one day the home-plate umpire didn't show up for an industrial-league softball game. I was supposed to play in the game, but they needed an umpire, and without one we couldn't play. My dad was a well-respected umpire in the area, so I figured I'd give it a try.

What the hell? I said to myself. *There can't be that much to it.*

And I volunteered.

I took over behind the plate and fell in love with it. I didn't have any problems. Things went smoothly. Everyone was tickled to death to have someone behind the plate who seemed to know what he was doing.

After that, I would umpire every chance I could.

Umpiring, like so many things, is like a disease. Some people catch it. Others don't. I'm afraid I got it. Pretty soon I was umpiring three or four games a week. I had no idea at the time that it would become my life's work. Since I was in high school, I'd get paid under the table. After the game someone would come over and slip me a five-dollar bill. This was because of what happened to Jim Thorpe, who won all those medals in the Olympics. When the authorities found out he was paid to play semipro baseball, they came and took all his medals away. I wasn't about to take the chance that I would lose my college eligibility because I was getting paid to umpire.

What I found out early was that I wasn't doing it for the money. I was doing it for the love of the game. I appreciated the money, but I really *loved* what I was doing. As I went through my life, I could see that many of my fellow umpires—especially those in the major leagues—really hated their jobs. Once an umpire makes it to the majors, he's making a lot of money and isn't about to quit. That's the reason so many umpires drink.

— 8 —

It wasn't too long before my dad and I began umpiring together. He'd take the plate and I'd umpire the bases. The first professional game I ever worked with my dad was played in Mexicali, Mexico, about twelve miles from home, just across the border. Mexicali was in the Sunset League and they were playing Riverside, California. The regular umpires had been in a car wreck. Dad was available, but the other alternate umpire, Jack Tatum, a highway patrolman, was in Sacramento attending a conference.

"Come with me, Doug," Dad said. "They need an umpire. You can work this."

We drove to the Mexican border. You always left your car on the American side of the border, because if the Mexicali fans became enraged enough, they could just as easily set fire to your car as not.

Mexicali was leading Riverside by two full games when we went down there to umpire the final three games of the season.

Little did I know that in Mexicali I would be working games played between professionals. Dad worked three games behind the plate and I worked the bases. Riverside won the first two games. The last game, played at night, was the decider.

The ballpark was jammed. The Mexicali fans were drinking their beer. The score was close. In the ninth inning Mexicali was leading by a run with two on and two outs when a batter hit a ground ball to the infield. I was umpiring the bases and the throw to first was close, but I saw the Riverside runner's shoe hit the bag before I heard the slap of the ball into the glove, and I called the runner safe.

The crowd sounded like buzzing bees, and I wondered in all seriousness whether the Mexicali fans were going to rush out of the stands and lynch me.

Things got even uglier when the next batter hit the ball nine miles to win the game and the pennant for visiting Riverside. When Mexicali didn't score in the bottom of the ninth, we had a full-blown riot.

An army truck backed up to the clubhouse door, and Dad and I got in the back of the truck, which was covered by a green tarp that was protecting us from the food and objects that were being thrown by the Mexicali fans. Soldiers lay on the floor of the truck with their rifles with bayonets sticking out the bottom of the tarp to prevent anyone from jumping onto the truck and attacking us. The driver floored it, and we sped out of there and headed for the border.

It was exciting. I had never seen anything like it and it served me well. I had kept my cool. Looking back, if the army hadn't been there to save us, we easily could have ended up dead. Those Mexicans were crazy—and crazy about baseball.

I saw that I had a knack for the job. I was born to officiate.

— 9 —

I played on the El Centro High School basketball team, and we were one of the first run-and-gun offenses in the United States. When I was first in high school, there was no such thing as a fast break. You got the ball, passed it out, and everyone trotted to the far end of the court to set up a play while the defense set itself. You passed the ball around until you saw an opening. There was no time clock. There was no rush, so you just passed it and passed it and passed it. When you saw an opening, you threw it to the open man, and he took a shot. A typical score was 20–17.

My junior year we had a terrible coach. We lost a couple of practice games at the start of the season, and he walked off, packed up, and left. Coach Farrell, who was the junior-varsity football coach, volunteered for the job and took it over. Coach Farrell was the one who came up with our run-and-gun offense. He worked us to death to get us in shape so we could play it, and we went on to win the California State championship.

At six foot two I was the team's center. I'd take the ball off the rebound, fire it to Babe Henry on the sideline, and then I'd break to the right. Babe would throw the ball to Red Gresham across court, and I'd race down to the other end, and we'd have a three-on-two and score. Before we knew it, we were winning games 40–25.

We played in short gyms where you had to throw your hands up to stop from hitting the wall after you scored a layup. The league would send short, round fellows to referee our games, and these fat little guys couldn't keep up with us as we fast-breaked down the court. We all thought, *These guys are terrible.* I said to myself, *I sure can do a better job than that.* I later went on to officiate in high school, college, and two pro leagues: the American Basketball League and the American Basketball Association.

No doubt in my mind basketball was my best sport. I played against guys who were six foot six and six foot seven, and I would outjump and outhustle them. I left their jockstraps hanging from the rafters.

I was sure I was going to get a college scholarship in basketball. Looking back, chances are if I had gotten one, I never would have become an umpire. I was invited by the coach at the University of California to visit the campus. He said he was thinking about giving me a scholarship. He took me over to their gym, and I couldn't believe what an old flophouse it was. You talk about a terrible gym for a college. But California was a good team. It was in the finals of the NCAA championship in 1946, and I was excited to come and work out for him.

I went up against a couple of their players and after we finished, he said to me, "Son, you have no left hand."

In other words, he saw that I didn't dribble or pass with my left hand.

I shrugged my shoulders and went back home. It didn't bother me. I ended up enrolling and playing football, basketball, and baseball at El Centro Junior College. I was sure I was going to get at least one scholarship offer, but March became April, and no offers came. I told myself, *Fuck it,* and in a rage and a feeling of self-pity I quit school and eloped with my high school sweetheart.

— 10 —

I was very much in love. I was crazy about her. I was a freshman at El Centro Junior College and Joan Manning was a senior at El Centro High School. She was my high school sweetheart. One of my friends bet me that we wouldn't go to Yuma, Arizona, and get married.

"Yes, I will," I said.

"Bet you won't," he replied. "Bet you five dollars."

"The hell I won't," I said. I probably shouldn't have.

Joan and I were driving around at night on a date. We were about sixty miles from Yuma, Arizona, which—according to the *Guinness Book of World Records*—is the sunniest place on earth. It's also the place where my first true love and I were married.

We went before the justice of the peace, got married, and drove home. The next day I went to her home and knocked on the door. Her father answered.

Being the honest guy that I am, I said to her father, "Cliff, I want you to know something. We've run away, and Joan and I have gotten married. But we have not completed the marriage. We've had no sex. I want you to know this in case you want us to annul this."

Her father wasn't happy.

"Get the fuck off my porch," is what he said to me. I guess he was angry. But he didn't tell us to get an annulment. In hindsight, I wish he had.

Unfortunately for the marriage, Joan liked to live high on the hog. We rented a nice house, and right after we got married she proceeded to fill it with expensive furniture, a newfangled refrigerator, and a phonograph and music that we paid for on credit. We didn't have much money and we ran up a huge debt. We were in love. She was a great gal. We were having a baby. I gave her everything she asked for.

One day I took stock. I believed in frugality—something else I inherited from my dad—and I suddenly realized how horribly in debt I was and that just ate at me. There was nothing I could do about it but quit college and go to work to pay it off.

My timing couldn't have been worse. After I quit college I received eight scholarship offers. USC, UCLA, and the University of Nevada all wanted me to come and play basketball. My grades were good; I had a B average. But I had quit school, gotten married, and taken on two jobs. A lot of guys would have skipped out on their debts, taken their wife, and headed for school—but again, it was a question of integrity. I had forged my destiny, and I wasn't about to go back.

— 11 —

As I said, the large debt we had rung up just ate at me, so I went to work on the night shift for a company called Arden Farms, which was a milk company. I had to be at work at two in the morning, and I would load milk and unload ice cream off the trucks that came down from San Diego, and then I loaded the ice cream onto milk trucks that went from house to house delivering products from Arden Farms. After my shift was over at ten a.m. I would then go pump gas at a local gas station. Then I'd go home, sleep, get something to eat, and head for the Arden Farms job again.

I was never home. After two years, sad to say, our marriage broke up. I got out of debt, but I had lost a wife—who, as you will see, then proceeded to make my life as miserable as she could make it.

I then took a job working for Eddie Maljin, the lettuce king of El Centro. His company boxed lettuce and shipped it to Chicago. One day Mr. Maljin said that if I would go to Hollywood and try out for the movies—and if he could be my manager—he would pay for singing and dancing lessons.

It could have changed my life, but at age twenty-two I didn't see a future in it for me.

"No," I told him, "that's not my thing."

For two years I worked Mr. Maljin's farm. I would get to the fields and climb on a tractor before sunup and I'd leave at sundown. From farming I learned important lessons in life: You have to accept the fact that the job has to get done and you have to be patient. If you want the vegetables to thrive in time for harvest, you had better be in that lettuce field at five o'clock in the morning. You got out and had to wait until the sun warmed the ice off the lettuce plants. The first thing you did was reach underneath the lettuce to see if there was any ice on the leaf. If there was, then you would have to wait. You felt again, and if it was still icy, you would wait some more. Once the ice melted, you had one day to pick the crop, whether it was lettuce or carrots.

It was a brutal existence. I worked in 125-degree heat in the summer. The dust would come off those front wheels and blow across my face. From sunup to sundown in the winter you could do 180 acres, either cultivating or cutting all the weeds down, getting the soil ready for planting, seeding, or putting the plants into the ground. I would drink a ten-gallon bottle of water a day. I gurgled when I walked.

"How do I get around having to drink ten gallons of water a day?" I asked a friend.

"Try this," he said.

He handed me a package of chewing tobacco. It wasn't long before I became addicted to it. I was so addicted that I chewed tobacco while refereeing basketball games. I'd take an empty pack and fill it with Kleenex, and I'd spit into that. I chewed the stuff for years, until the day in 1997 when I was diagnosed with throat cancer.

I finally quit farming when I got a better job. I was hired by the Southern California Gas Company as a meter reader. I hustled, and by noon I would have all the meters read in Imperial Valley, and I made sure they were read 100 percent the way my bosses wanted them read. It wasn't long before they made me a new-construction representative at a raise in pay. It was very good money, but after a year I wasn't given another raise, and I asked my sales-department boss why.

"Because you don't have a college education," he said.

"What the hell has that got to with anything?" I wanted to know.

"I'm college educated," he said. "Without a college degree, you'll never get any further."

"Fine," I said. "You have my seven days' notice."

"What does that mean?" he asked angrily.

"I quit," I told him. "I'm going back to college."

CHAPTER 3

HARD KNOCKS AT COLLEGE

— 1 —

About this time a process server showed up at my door. My wife, Joan, was suing me for divorce. She was tired of being left alone so much. We had stopped being civil. She was barely twenty-one, and having a son at such a young age had crimped her fun.

We went to a lawyer and drew up papers, and as part of the agreement she gave me our son, Doug Jr., who was an infant.

I was thrilled. My mom and dad agreed to help me take care of him. Mom would watch him.

Then Joan's parents got involved.

"No mother gives up her child," her mother told her.

Before I knew it, the sheriff came and took my son away while I was at work. I was devastated when he came and took my child.

I tried to fight it, but the law was on the side of the mother and there was nothing I could do about it.

It was so unfair. Joan hadn't even wanted the child. In addition, the judge ruled I had to pay her a burdensome thousand-dollar-a-month child support. He ruled that I could visit my son one day a week.

I had to get away from her and El Centro. I was determined to go back to college.

Timing is everything. I was umpiring a Little League game when I got to talking with one of the coaches about my wanting to go to college. He was a noted eye doctor in El Centro, and when I told him I had quit my job and was thinking of moving to San Diego, he said, "If you do, contact Charlie Smith at San Diego State."

Charlie Smith was the San Diego State baseball coach.

I went to see Coach Smith on a Thursday.

"I don't have time to talk to you today," he said. "Come back on Saturday."

When I returned I could see he had all my school records in front of him. He found out I had lettered in football, basketball, and baseball for three years, and most important, he learned I had a B average.

"Come with me," he said. "Let me show you around campus."

During our walk I told him I was interested in joining the umpires' association in San Diego.

He apparently had bigger plans for me.

After he showed me the campus and the baseball field, we

walked into the college bookstore. He stacked up a pile of books and said, "Here we go."

"What's this all about?" I asked.

"You have just registered at San Diego State," he said. "If you want to, you're going to play baseball for me, and if you do, I will give you a partial scholarship."

It wasn't nearly enough to cover expenses because of the high child support I was paying, but it was something, and I accepted gladly.

— 2 —

I transferred to San Diego State College as a sophomore in January 1955 and immediately joined the baseball team. I played two years of varsity baseball, two years of varsity football, and a year of junior-varsity basketball. My sophomore year I played second, short, and third, and my junior year I became the starting catcher. In our first game, Noel Mickelsen was our starting pitcher against Stanford. Noel eventually made it to Triple-A in the Pacific Coast League. In the first inning a batter flew out, and two struck out, but our catcher couldn't hold him, so instead of there being three outs we were behind 2–0 and the bases were loaded with one out.

I was the second-string catcher, and I was sitting in the bullpen when Coach Smith called over to me.

"Harvey, can you catch him?" he wanted to know.

"I can try," I said.

I had caught fast-pitch softball, and if you can catch that, you can catch anything. I went behind the plate and ended up catching almost all of our games that year.

I was a line-drive hitter. I could hit and I could bunt. When the season started I asked Coach Smith, "Who won the batting title last year for us?" He said our top batter the year before had hit .360.

"I'm going to beat that," I said, and I did each year. I batted an average of .378 the two years I was there.

We had a pretty darn good team. My senior year we traveled to the University of Arizona for a two-game series. Arizona was undefeated at the time, and we won one of the games. We were housed underneath the bleachers of the football stadium, and after our win a bunch of us snuck out and mounted a panty raid at one of the sorority houses. We were caught in the act and sent back to our quarters.

We had some fun. We used to drive to our games, to L.A., Santa Barbara, to Cal Poly in San Luis Obispo, and to Fresno, and often heading north we'd go through Laguna Beach, where an old ne'er-do-well stood on one of the busiest street corners directing traffic. I had seen him the first time through, and I thought it would be fun to buy a water cannon and soak him down as we drove past. Then, when we got to Santa Barbara, our team took half the second floor of the Santa Barbara Hotel, and we all went out and bought water guns and had gigantic water fights.

I wasn't a natural student, and when we'd go on the road I would take my books with me and spend much of the time studying. I was also worried about my eligibility, and I studied when I could to keep from falling behind.

After my second season I was offered a chance at pro ball.

"Son, we'd like to sign you to a contract."

"To where?"

"You start in Florida."

"I'm not going to Florida," I told him.

I had a sick mother, and I wanted to see my infant son as much as possible.

Instead of going to play pro baseball, I stayed in school. I played a second season of football when I returned in the fall. I played second-string halfback on offense and was a starting linebacker and back on defense. I could hold my own.

— 3 —

To pay my child support and the rest of the tuition not covered by my scholarship, I had to work. Once again I was on a merry-go-round. I would go to class from nine until noon, then I'd play ball for San Diego State. After baseball practice I was a one-man grounds crew/clubhouse boy. I'd rake the pitcher's mound and the batter's box, drag the infield by hand, then take a shower, wipe down the showers, and gather up all the wet towels. Then I'd take them to be laundered. I'd then turn off all the showers and close up the locker room. I'd head to my room, get something to eat, study for an hour maybe, and then head to my second job at the Safeway supermarket, where I'd stock shelves for two hours. Then I'd report to my third job at the Playhouse Bar on El Cajon Boulevard in San Diego. The bar was owned by a disabled fellow by the name of Monroe "Bookie" Clark. When Bookie was a student at USC, he would broker the athletes' extra game tickets. He was a hustler, and he hired me as a bouncer who checked IDs at this shit-hole of a bar in east San Diego. I was also the cleanup guy.

The place would close at two in the morning, and every night I'd restock the bar, mop the floors, run the vacuum, and usually lie down and fall asleep. Every night the place stank of stale beer and cigarettes, and it was my job to make sure it smelled nice in the morning. I even had to clean the toilets. It was the worst job I ever had.

Around seven in the morning there'd be a knock on the door from a customer who wanted a drink. I'd get up, pour him a drink, write down how much it was and who ordered it, then go back to mopping the floor and scrubbing the bar. By then it was time to head back to San Diego State.

As you can see, I wasn't afraid of doing a little hard work.

— 4 —

My college career ended after I broke my leg playing football and our new football coach took away my half scholarship.

In the fall of my junior year I was playing defensive halfback. I went to make a tackle and was hit from behind by one of my teammates. I heard something down in my leg that sounded like the ripping of cloth. I trotted over to the doctor on the sideline.

He felt around and said, "There's nothing wrong with it."

"Tape it up," I said, and I went back into the game.

The other team ran a play sweeping around their left end, and I went charging in there, and for a second time a teammate hit me from behind, and this time I knew I was seriously injured.

"Coach," I said. "Something's very wrong. My leg isn't right."

A teammate of mine on the baseball team, Jim Pyle, was standing on the sideline, and the coach asked him to take me to the hospital.

We got in Jim's car and drove to the local hospital, where they took X-rays of my ankle.

"Nothing is wrong," they concluded.

"Okay, let's get back to the ball game, Jim."

I could barely walk, but they said I was okay, so I was willing to give it a try.

We took the elevator down to the main floor, and we began

walking out to Jim's car when a nurse came running over to say they wanted to take more X-rays.

This time they took X-rays farther up the leg, and they discovered that my leg bone had been split in half. The ends of the bone were inches apart.

They put me in a hard cast up to my ass, and I stayed in that cast for twenty weeks.

At the end of the football season Bill Schutte, my head coach, retired, and he was replaced by Paul Governali, an all-American quarterback at Columbia University and a real asshole whom all the players hated. He was a horseshit coach. Governali came in and took away my half scholarship and gave it to another player.

I would never forgive the son of a bitch. He knew the trouble I was in and he didn't care. He was supposed to be all-everything, a big name, and he was just a bad guy. Years later I ran into his ex-wife. When I told her I didn't have much respect for him, she said, "That son of a bitch didn't have anybody's respect."

"I can understand why you divorced him," I told her. "I would have if I could have."

— 5 —

In addition to owing my ex-wife alimony, I also owed about $800 to a man who owned a gas station and fixed my car. I decided to drop out of school and work to pay my alimony and pay off my debts.

I asked the gas-station owner if I could work for him to pay off my debt, and he agreed. In addition to my bar job, I also took a job as a guard with the Aztec Security Company. Even though I had a cast up to my ass, I was able to wear a uniform, stand there, and take IDs at events.

Before long I was able to pay off most of my debts. Also helping me were my ex-wife's futile, self-destructive attempts to shake me down for more money. You think you know somebody. It's like she had become an animal, and all she wanted to do was rip me apart. You say to yourself, *What did I ever do to her?* And you go in and try to be decent and you say to her, "Let's try to work this out"—and holy shit, all of a sudden, wow, she wants your hide.

Four times she demanded I appear in court for a hearing, interrupting my college and ball playing, and four times I had to drive from San Diego to El Centro to go before a judge.

The first time I came to court, the judge said I was being charged with not having paid my child support.

"Wait a minute, Your Honor," I said. "Can I show you something?"

"Sure," he said.

I reached into my pocket, walked up to the judge, and pulled out all of my receipts.

"There's not one missing, is there, Your Honor?" I said.

"No, there isn't."

After I laid out the receipts, he pounded his gavel a couple of times and said, "From now on, he will pay half as much."

I went back to school, and darned if she didn't do this to me three more times. She didn't even show up herself. But each time the judge cut my child support until I was paying only $50 a month. By trying to hurt me, she hurt herself.

The saddest part of the whole affair was that my son was the greatest kid in the world. After she took him back, she did nothing but bad-mouth me, and before long she made a hard-nose red-ass out of him. After that, no matter what I did, he thought I was wrong, and she thought I was wrong. Finally I said, "Fuck them both," and we had a real falling-out.

When he was in his twenties, Douglas Lee Harvey got into trouble with drugs and alcohol. He was lost for the next thirty years. It broke my heart. He was so far gone that he wanted nothing more to do with his mother or me. At various times during his addiction Joy and I tried the best we could to get help for him, but he wasn't at all interested in getting help. He didn't care, and after a while, we didn't either. We knew we could only help him if he wanted to help himself.

Only after he got cancer and was in the hospital did I go see him. My wife talked me into going, and we settled things. That was the good part of it. And then, sadly, Doug died. It was heartbreaking. God rest his troubled soul.

CHAPTER 4

A PERFECT INSPIRATION

— 1 —

I was sitting in the Playhouse Bar waiting for the World Series to come on TV. It was October 8, 1956, and the New York Yankees were playing the Brooklyn Dodgers in the World Series, so I stuck around the bar to watch game 5 with a few of the shot-and-beer regulars I knew. The game was played during the day, as were all the World Series games back then. Because of the three-hour time difference, the World Series games usually started at ten in the morning in California. The regulars had been drinking; I'd had a few myself, and I was sitting there wondering what I was going to do with the rest of my life.

I was twenty-six years old, going nowhere.

Yankee pitcher Don Larsen was making short shrift of the

Dodgers. He was holding them without a hit. As the game moved into the late innings, I began to focus on Babe Pinelli, the umpire behind the plate. I began thinking to myself: *I've worked a lot of jobs, but none gives me the satisfaction that umpiring does.* I had umpired high school and college games in El Centro since I was sixteen, but I had never considered it as a profession before then.

As I watched Don Larsen and his perfect game unfold, I had an epiphany.

"Well, I'll be a son of a bitch. I know what I want to be," I said out loud to my buddies sitting with me at the bar.

"What's that?" they asked.

"I'm going to be a major league umpire."

"Hey," said the guy sitting next to me, "Harvey here says he's going to be a major league umpire."

"Yeah, right, Harv," came the response. "Sure you are."

The bunch of them started laughing at me, and I became so upset, so angry at their reaction—their making sport of me—that I got up and left.

Don Larsen pitched his perfect game, of course, and six years later those same guys who were with me at the bar would watch me work my first major league game. Two years after that, I was working in Jocko Conlan's crew.

Those guys should've known better. Never tell me I can't do something, because I'll prove you wrong every time.

— 2 —

I couldn't afford umpire school, the usual way men make it to the big leagues as umpires. I began writing letters to the presidents of all the minor leagues, from the International League and the American Association on down to the D leagues. I must have written fifty letters trying to break into the pros as an umpire. I received no replies. Meanwhile, I kept working as many amateur and semipro games as I could.

I was umpiring in San Diego, doing a semipro game. I had just arrived for the game and was assigned to work the bases. We were using a two-man system. The other fellow, a local San Diego schoolteacher, was supposed to work home plate. He slapped his shin guards on and went, "Uh-oh . . . my God."

"What's wrong with you?" I asked.

"It's just a stitch," he said.

"Can you stand up?" I asked.

"Yeah," he said, "but it hurts when I bend over."

"You work the bases and I'll work the plate," I said.

It was no big deal. I went to my little DeSoto, slapped on my shin guards, got out there, and called balls and strikes.

About the third inning, the catcher said, "Hey, kid, you're doing a pretty good job."

"I appreciate that," I said.

"Especially for an important game," he added.

"What do you mean, an important game?"

"You don't know, do you?" he said. "This is the final game of the five-game series between Los Angeles County and San Diego County for the Southern California baseball championship."

"Swell; that's nice," I said. To me there are no important games, because every game is an important game.

I guess it was big to him. We went back to work, and in the next half inning the catcher said, "By the way, was the umpire at first base supposed to work the plate?"

"Yeah," I said.

"He was supposed to work the final game for three straight years, and he hasn't worked the plate yet," he said.

"No kidding?"

We finished the game, no problems. I wasn't in too good of a mood and walked over to the other umpire.

The guy said, "Hey, Harv, thanks."

"No problem," I said.

I started taking off my gear. I didn't feel like talking to him, I was so mad. But in my life, the important moments have often come when least expected. It turned out that the other umpire did me one of the biggest favors I ever received. Had he not changed places with me that day, it's very possible I would never have become a major league umpire. Because after the game, a guy wearing a straw hat came up to me and said, "Young fella, you worked a pretty good game."

"I'm glad you realized that," I said, still pissed off because I felt the other umpire had suckered me into taking the plate that day.

"I'm Johnny Moore, a scout for the Milwaukee Braves," he said. "Did you ever think about turning professional?"

"Yeah," I said. "I've written about fifty letters, and I can't get anybody to answer one. They want me to go to umpire school, and I can't afford it. I broke my left leg playing football at San Diego State and was in a cast for twenty-seven weeks. Now I'm working to pay an eight-hundred-dollar gasoline bill that I ran up after Coach Governali took away my scholarship and job on campus."

"You've had it pretty bad," he said. "If I can get you a job, do you want to work as an umpire in pro baseball?"

"I certainly would," I said. "In a heartbeat."

He handed me a card.

"If you don't hear from me in a week, call me at that number."

Had I been working the bases that day, I doubt he would have noticed me, even though I considered myself the best base umpire ever to walk out onto a ball field. At the time, I considered myself a mediocre plate umpire, but on the bases I was outstanding. I settled everything with a kind word.

When the man in the straw hat said he was a scout for the Milwaukee Braves, I really wasn't sure whether he was pulling my leg or not, but two weeks later I received a telegram informing me I was on the roster of umpires for the California League, Class C, at a salary of $250 a month.

It was the greatest day of my life, so far.

CHAPTER 5

ROOTLESS IN THE MINORS

— 1 —

Class C was starting close to the bottom. Two umpires worked a game as a team. In the California League we umpired games all over the San Joaquin Valley. The first year, my partner owned a car, and he was paid five cents a mile to travel to the games. I lived out of my suitcase. I didn't rent an apartment or go back to a place to live. There was no home base.

After a game was over, we'd grab a couple of fifteen-cent hamburgers and then drive a couple hundred miles or more to small towns up and down central California, like Modesto, Visalia, and Bakersfield. During the summer it was hot as hell, and the fields were more like cow pastures—rough and unforgiving, like the fans who wanted your hide every night. For this punishment (I loved it), I was told I was getting $50 more than most of the California League umpires, because I had come so highly recommended. It was a good thing that I was single and had paid off almost all of my debts.

My second year I was paired with another umpire, a young guy with a wife and daughter who one day broke down and confessed to me that he was so broke he didn't have enough money to rent an apartment and feed his family. He was only making $200 a month and wasn't making ends meet.

As a child I was taught the importance of empathy, to picture yourself in the shoes of the other guy. After he spilled his tale of woe, I felt for him, and so I gave him almost half my salary so he could bring his wife and daughter on the road with us. I was single. My only living expense was my room, because I knew that after every game the home team would provide the umpires with a sandwich or a hamburger, and that was all I needed to get by. I was counting on the home team's after-game sustenance for my survival.

We were working a game in Visalia and there was a situation on the field where I ejected Visalia's manager and one of their better players, and Visalia lost the ball game by a run. That night after the game, we arrived at our dressing room only to find that no food had been left for my partner and me.

"Where's our food?" I asked the batboy.

"We were told not to bring it, Mr. Harvey," the boy said.

This was retaliation by the Visalia general manager for my calling a play against his team and ejecting the manager and one of his players.

"Okay, thanks," I said.

I didn't get mad. This was one trait that separated me from most of the other umpires I knew. Very early I learned that getting mad didn't accomplish very much. We had to go into town to get a bite to eat at our own expense.

Before the game the next day, my partner and I went to the office of the Visalia general manager to get the baseballs for the game. We always picked up two dozen balls: a dozen and a half new balls and a half dozen gently used balls from the game before.

In front of the general manager, I picked up the used balls and put them aside.

"Give me six more new ones," I ordered.

"Why?" he wanted to know.

"Give me six new ones," I repeated.

"What are you doing, Harv?" he asked.

"As long as you think I'm not worth a sandwich," I said, "we're going to do this every night. Give me six new balls." I was going to make him pay. He got the message. After each game at Visalia, there were a couple of hamburgers, a hot dog, and a drink waiting for us. We ate like kings.

It became one of my mantras: *Don't get mad. Get even.*

— 2 —

When I started working in C Ball—and this was true throughout my umpiring career—I was often told, "If you want to make it in the major leagues, you have to have a pitcher's strike zone." In other words, you have to open up your strike zone a little bit. In theory, if you give the pitchers the close ones instead of calling balls, the pitchers will be less likely to bitch and moan, and the game will go faster.

I categorically refused to do that. The rule book determined what was a strike and what was a ball, and I was determined that I would strictly go by what the rule book had to say.

Screw it, I said to myself, *I'll take their arguments and stand on my own.*

During my entire career, I was a great believer in fairness. I absolutely was fair. Opening up the strike zone by definition means that you're cheating for the pitcher, and I don't know how to cheat in any direction. I absolutely made the ball touch the plate if I was going to call it a strike. And of course it had to be the right height.

When I first began umpiring in the minors, a couple of the other umpires asked me, "Who do you know in the major leagues?"

"Nobody," I said. Which was true. I had no contacts at all.

"You might as well hang it up," I was told. "You're not going to make it. You don't have a chance in hell."

I ignored them. I knew how good I was in this job. No, I

hadn't gone to umpire school, and no, I didn't have any contacts to rely on. What I was sure of was that talent and hard work would overcome any of that. I was confident my chance would come. What I needed was the patience to wait for that chance to arrive.

It wasn't all that easy working in the low minors. A lot of guys who were pretty good umpires didn't make it. It's a tough grind, really tough. There were a lot of times when I said to myself, *I don't think I can do this anymore.*

The longest drive in the California League was Bakersfield to Reno. It was 411 miles, two-lane highways, one going each way. It was highway to Sacramento and then mountains all the way to Reno. We would leave at midnight and arrive in Reno when the sun was coming up.

Say we finished a night game in Bakersfield. You showered and you stopped and got a sandwich or something to eat and then you left town at one o'clock in the morning for the long drive to Reno.

These were dangerous two-lane highways all the way. You just drove as far as you could, and if the other guy was awake, he drove as far as he could. Sometimes I think back and really don't know how any of us made it without falling asleep at the wheel and killing ourselves.

One time we were in Bakersfield. It was 1959, and I had just finished working a doubleheader. We were changing clothes in the dressing room and there was a knock on the door.

"You worked a helluva game," this fella said.

He introduced himself as Al Widmar of the Philadelphia Phillies. He said he was scouting for the Phillies and had noticed my talents.

"Now I have two suggestions, if you want to make it to the majors," he said. "You gotta dye your hair, and you gotta stop chewing tobacco." My hair had started turning gray when I was fifteen. I've always been gray. And I had been chewing tobacco ever since I began farming in Imperial Valley, where it was so dry I needed the wet chewing tobacco to keep me lubricated.

"Let me tell you something," I said. "If they don't want a gray-haired, tobacco-chewing umpire, they're not getting me."

Whether I was capable of calling balls and strikes and outs seemed more relevant. So was knowing the game.

I worked like hell. When I went into the California League, I was about six foot two, 170 pounds, good-looking fella, liked a few drinks, liked to toddle a few. My partners would always say after games, "Hey, let's go down to the Kern River. There are women down there. C'mon, we'll go down and chase the women for the afternoon." I mean, it was hotter than hell in Bakersfield in the summertime.

The guys would try to get me to carouse, but I'd always say, "Nah, I've got things I gotta do," like laundry or call my mom.

I was lying to them. They were probably the only lies I ever told in my life. More important than carousing and drinking, I felt, was studying the rule book one to two hours every day I was in the minor leagues. I figured by my doing that, more than any other thing, it would get me to the major leagues quicker—other than the fact that I was a good umpire. One to two hours every day I studied. I never missed a day. And that's why I always knew what I was talking about when it came to the rules.

To me the rule book is the Bible of baseball. I would read that book in hot hotel rooms without air-conditioning and nothing but a small fan. I memorized every word. I knew if I was to be an umpire who was respected by the managers and players, I would have to know the game inside and out. My goal was to be more knowledgeable about the way the game was played than anyone on the field. And you know what? It paid off, though it made for a rather lonely, barren existence. After tutoring myself on the rule book, there was little else for me to do until game time. I didn't have any money to go anyplace. I didn't have transportation. My partner had the car. So what was I going to do? And that was tough. I was out there on a shoestring doing the best I could, and it wasn't easy. But you have to know Doug Harvey. I had set my mind to make it, and I stubbornly refused to change. I just went at it, day after day.

But it was my knowledge of the rules that helped get me noticed. In my second year in C ball in the California League there was a runner on second base. The runner on second broke for third. Everyone hollered, "There he goes," and the pitcher quickly threw the ball to third base. The runner, seeing he was a dead duck, stopped, turned, and slid back into second base.

The manager of the team at bat was Buddy Kerr, the former New York Giants shortstop. Buddy came running out.

"Harvey, I've got you," he said.

"Oh really, Buddy," I said.

"Yes, I do," he said. "That's a balk."

"Beg your pardon?" I said.

"That's a balk," Buddy repeated. "The rule says you cannot throw to an unoccupied base. It's a balk."

"Buddy, I'm proud of you," I said.

He had the dumbest look on his face.

"What the fuck do you mean, you're proud of me?" he asked.

"To think somebody in this godforsaken league besides me is reading the rule book," I said. "I'm really proud of you, Buddy."

"I don't care," he said. "It's a balk, Harvey. Move him over."

"Your biggest problem, Buddy," I said, "is you don't know which rule it is. It's Rule 805. There are thirteen ways in which to balk: Rule 805, sections A through M. You should have kept reading, Buddy. There's a comma there, and it says, *Except for the express purpose of making a play*. Now, Buddy, where was the runner going?"

"To third base," he said sheepishly.

"Where did he throw?"

"To third base." He paused. "Goddamnit, Harvey."

"Get away from me, Buddy," I told him.

And Buddy walked back to the dugout.

— 3 —

One of the other managers I had in the California League was Dave Bristol, one of the real assholes of the world. Johnny Edwards, a catcher who went up to the Cincinnati Reds with him, was hitting when the opposing pitcher hit Edwards in the head with a fastball. Edwards went down like a big old oak tree. *Bam*, he hit the deck.

I walked over to see how Edwards was. Bristol came over, slapped Edwards in the face, and said, “Are you all right?”

“Yeah, I’m all right,” Edwards said.

“Don’t you want to have him looked at?” I asked Bristol.

“You mind your goddamn business,” was his reply.

Edwards walked to first base.

I turned around and walked back to my position in the infield, because we were working a two-man system.

In the middle of the inning I called time. Edwards had fallen to his knees and was obviously in trouble. He was taken to the hospital, and it turned out he had a bad concussion. In those days, if you weren’t dizzy, you played. But that was typical of Bristol.

— 4 —

It was in the minor leagues that I began to develop some of my rules for how managers and players should conduct themselves with respect to arguing with umpires. One of my most hard-and-fast rules was that I would not tolerate a manager or player calling me a name.

Managers and players know well the magic words when it comes to getting tossed. But my feeling was that being an umpire is like being a policeman in civilized society. You don't go around calling policemen names unless you want to get arrested. I wanted managers and players to understand that you don't call the umpires names, either.

One day, when I was umpiring in the California League, there was a close play, and the manager of the team came out to argue with me. After he had his say, I told him he had better get away from me.

"You're going to get tossed if you don't," I warned him.

He turned and started to walk away, and as he did, he put his hand behind him and made a shooing motion. In a voice loud enough for me to hear, he said, "You're a fucking hot dog."

And I tossed him from the game.

He stopped and came back to me and asked, "What the hell was that for?"

"I don't call you names," I said. "You don't call me a hot dog."

"All I said was that you were a hot dog," he answered.

"That's a name," I said. "You're gone."

After a while the managers and players came to understand that if you called me a name—and it didn't have to be a swearword—you'd be tossed.

— 5 —

After two years in the Class C California League, I was offered a chance to go up to Class B, the Carolina League. I had gotten a $25-a-month raise in pay to $275 a month, and the Carolina League wanted me to take a pay cut.

"Why should I do that?" I asked.

"Because it's a promotion to Class B," I was told.

"I don't give a damn what it is," I said. "My mother lives here in California, and I'm not going across the United States to make less money."

"You'll never make it with that attitude," I was told.

I should have bet him that I would.

CHAPTER 6

JOY

— 1 —

During my second year in the California League I met the love of the rest of my life. We met at a ballpark, Sam Lynn Stadium in Bakersfield, California. The ballpark was off one of the main drags of Bakersfield near the river. It faced west, which was really terrible for afternoon ball games.

I was standing at first base, and between innings I was looking into the stands. I saw this pair of blue hips walking up the stands with her back to me, wearing a blue pair of shorts and a white peasant blouse. I watched this girl carrying a tray, and when she turned around and came back toward me, I gulped.

Holy cow, I thought. *That's not too bad.*

Even though I couldn't get her out of my mind, I didn't mess up the ball game, and the next day I went looking for her. I learned that she was single, her name was Joy Glascock, and she was working at the ballpark selling scorecards and seat cushions before the game and refreshments during the game. She was making money to go back to Mills College, a hoity-toity all-girls college in Oakland.

When I approached her, she was saying good-bye to one of the other girls working with her. She was straightening her money, getting it organized for when the game started.

She was standing by a light pole, and when I saw she was about to walk away, I stuck out my arm to keep her there.

I made up a story to get her attention.

"Joy, what's it been?" I said to her. "Six years? How have you been? I didn't hardly recognize you."

She had no idea who I was, of course, and I kept on like we knew each other. She said hello, and I said, "I have to go to work. How about you and me getting reacquainted? Let's have a cup of coffee after the ball game."

She agreed to meet me for coffee.

Joy checked around and found out who I was. She knew she'd been scammed. And when the game was over, I looked around and she was nowhere to be found. Apparently she had gone home. What I didn't know was that she had gotten a ride with her sister, who also worked at the park. When it took me awhile after the game to get ready, she decided I wasn't coming, and because the ballpark wasn't in the nicest part of town and because it was a long way home, she left with her sister.

The next night I accosted her again, and I jumped all over her because I wasn't used to being stood up. She apologized, lamely explaining that she just hadn't waited long enough and so she went home.

"I'll be glad to go out with you tonight," she said.

And then I stood *her* up.

We were supposed to meet after the game. Her sister left, and she hung around. Everyone dressed and left, and the lights in the park were going out. I could see her leaving the ballpark, walking alone down the road toward a little honky-tonk bar where she intended to call her sister to come and pick her up.

When I pulled up beside her, she was mad as a wet hen.

"So how does it feel?" I shouted out the window.

And there, in the middle of the parking lot, Joy and I had a flaming fight.

Finally I convinced her to get in the car.

Once we got over the fight, we had a really good time.

That's how it started.

We began dating, and I told Joy I had been married before and wasn't interested in getting married again.

"That's fine," she said. "I've just broken an engagement with a guy, and I'm not interested in getting serious either."

We made an agreement that we were just going to date for companionship and fun, that we weren't going to get serious, because she was going back to college and I was traveling almost every day all across the state of California, umpiring.

I told her I was on an eight-year plan for my career. I figured going from C ball, to B ball, to A ball, to AA ball, to AAA ball, and then to the major leagues would take about eight years, and if I didn't make it by then, I would do something else.

Before expansion there were only sixteen major league teams. There were perhaps thirty-five umpires in each league. Back then, some umpires worked in the minor leagues for twenty years. It isn't like it is today, when after a certain number of years they boot you out. To get one of those spots someone had to die, almost. Plus the fact nobody was making any money after they made it. I think the top umpires were getting paid $17,000 a year in the majors when I first arrived. It was barely a living.

A year later I woke up one morning and said to her, "I better break this thing off."

"Why?" she asked.

"Because I'm getting serious."

"I am too," was what she said.

What was ironic was that Joy had refused to date the minor league baseball players because they made no money, and for the most part their prospects were bleak. Being her father's daughter, she was looking for a husband with prospects. If only she had known what she was getting into! Even if I made it, this was no path to riches. Fortunately for me, Joy and I came from families where it was honorable to go out to work, make a living, and save and be careful how you spent your money. As we dated and got to know each other, we found we had a lot in common; a lot of value systems in common. She went back to college and I went on with my umpiring, and that winter I arrived at her home in Bakersfield and proposed.

Joy was a lovely girl. Her mother had me over to their house enough for me to know Joy was a good cook. She was in her last year of college, so I knew she was intelligent. I also knew she was industrious. When I met her she worked daytime for her dad at his shop, and at night she worked at the ballpark to help pay her college expenses. Her dad was paying her tuition. She had to pay the rest.

When we got engaged, she said she wanted to quit school to be with me, but I made her go back and finish.

"I have my schedule, and you have yours," I said. "Get your education."

She went on to graduate from Mills College, and we got married a year later.

Joy likes to say I married her for her money, because when we got married I had a hundred dollars and she had two hundred.

I told her, "Joy, I've played around and had a lot of fun. If you will have me for a husband, I promise you I don't need to mess around. My dad wasn't true to my mom, but I believe in marriage, and I will be true to you."

And that's the way we lived for more than half a century.

The marriage took place in Bakersfield, Joy's hometown, just after the baseball season ended. We had a Methodist wedding. The morning before the ceremony I went out and played golf with my brother Nolan, Jim Pyle, my best friend, and my father-in-law-to-be, who owned a lumber supply company. We were on the tenth hole when someone came racing out onto the golf course and told my father-in-law-to-be, "You better get your ass back to the house and dress." I can only think the message came from my future mother-in-law. He left. I was playing the best game of golf I had all year. I was nailing every shot, and pretty soon Nolan said, "Doug, I better go. I have things I have to do, and I have to pick up our other brothers."

Off he went. Jim and I were determined to finish the round. We almost made it. When we arrived at the eighteenth tee, we had only thirty-five minutes until the ceremony was scheduled to begin, and even though the church was on the same side of Bakersfield as the golf course, my motel room was on the other side of town.

Jim—who was to be the best man—and I busted our hump, speeding across town and speeding back, and we walked into the church with exactly four minutes to spare. Talk about grace under pressure. They started playing "Here Comes the Bride," and it wasn't long before I was married to a wonderful woman. She couldn't have been any better.

Joy had said to me, "You can invite up to fifty people." I didn't know fifty people in Bakersfield. I was from San Diego and I wasn't that sociable. I invited two managers from the California League. One was a good guy, honest and truthful. When he would come out to talk, he wasn't throwing crap at you just to get you mad. When I asked my wife-to-be if it would be all right to invite him, she agreed.

The other manager, whose last name was Perry, was the manager of the Dodgers' farm team. He was called the Little Buffalo, and I knew I was going to eject him one out of three times. He and I just did not get along.

"Send the son of a bitch an invitation," I told Joy. I never thought he'd come. I invited him as a joke, but the little prick showed up. As he came down the reception line, he told Joy, "I hope you can do something with that meathead. I can't do anything with him."

Joy and I drank champagne, and we headed out for a five-hour drive to Lake Tahoe. I was driving on a two-lane highway, and after about an hour we were in Fresno and I was too drunk to continue.

"This is it," I told her. "This is as far as I can go. No more."

I pulled in and we stayed the night. The next day we continued on to Reno.

I had good friends living in Reno. Their sons were batboys for the Reno Silver Sox, and they would come to the games and take us out to dinner afterward. When you're getting a salary of $212 a month and $180 a month in expense money for room and board, a good meal is a luxury. You have four helpings of everything, because in the minor leagues you're running half-starved.

After arriving in Reno we checked into a motel. We were having dinner with our friends the next night, and so Joy and I took $5 each and went into a casino to gamble a little bit. I was thirty and Joy was twenty-two. She had such a lovely face and was so fresh-looking that after we walked into the casino, security guards came over to us and hauled us into the office. They accused me of transporting underage girls over the Nevada border for indecent purposes. And they were deadly serious about it.

Neither one of us had our IDs. We had left them in the hotel room, and they wouldn't believe our story that we had just gotten married. They wouldn't believe Joy was twenty-two years old. They were sure she was a minor, that she was far too young to be gambling, and that I intended no good as far as she was concerned.

I did what I could to convince them I was an umpire in the California League.

"Goddamn, get a baseball fan in here. He can identify me."

I told them to call my friends, the parents of the batboys.

They called, and my friend assured the security guards that Joy was in fact twenty-two years old and that I wasn't smuggling young girls across the border.

That's the way we started our marriage.

After the guards released us, Joy and I took the $5 we each brought and gambled. Between the two of us we had two hundred and some dollars, and two hundred of it was Joy's. We used that money to rent hotel rooms and pay for gas from San Diego to Bakersfield to Tahoe and back to San Diego.

When we returned to San Diego I went to a fellow who sold real estate. I asked him, "What's the chance of renting me one of your apartments?"

"I can do that," he said.

"Here is my card," I said. "This is who I am. I don't have any money. I can't make a down payment. Will you put my wife and me up long enough for us to earn some money and pay you?"

He said he would.

I had worked for the Aztec Security Company when I was going to San Diego State, and I went back to the owner and asked him if he could use me as a security guard. He gave me a job working from eight in the evening until eight in the morning, guarding motor homes that were sitting outside Balboa Stadium. They were having a show there, and he needed someone to walk around and check the doors of the motor homes. Joy got in touch with some real estate people and got a job going in and cleaning out rooms when tenants moved out of their apartments. Together we made enough money to pay rent and have a few bucks in our pockets.

For most of my childhood I was short and scrawny, and it was only when I became college age that I grew to my present height of six foot two. When I met Joy, inside I still felt as though I was five foot four, and she had to explain to me, "You're a large person. You have to change the way you see yourself."

It's been fifty-two years now. I couldn't do without her. She's a wonderful woman.

— 2 —

In 1961 I was umpiring winter-league ball in Arizona—the Instructional League. It was like our honeymoon. Four clubs were down there, and there were four umpires working two games a day. There was a Texas League ump there and he was holding court. I had just gotten married three months before, and my wife, Joy, was there with me.

"There was never an umpire who was taken out of one of these Instructional Leagues in baseball," he said. "I've been to six of these. I know that no one is going to move ahead, so I advise you to go through the motions, collect the money, put in your month and a half, and get the hell out of here."

On the ride home my wife knew something was bothering me.

"What's the matter?" she asked.

"Joy," I said, "I don't know how to umpire like that man was talking about."

"My first advice to you as your wife," she said, "is that you should umpire the way you know how."

— 3 —

In 1961 I was umpiring in Phoenix in the Instructional League for rookies. In Arizona I continued to study the rules for at least an hour every day. Joy helped me. She would hold the rule book and I would recite the rules verbatim, including commas, periods, and parentheses. I was really focused on making it to the major leagues, and I was hoping with hard work, determination, and luck that the right people would notice. I knew scouts were there to see the ballplayers, but we found out that they also noticed the umpires.

Some of the Instructional League umpires had been there for years, and one of them said to me, "Why are you knocking yourself out? Nobody ever gets promoted from this league. We're just here to pick up our paychecks."

That was also true of some of the ballplayers, I noticed. They knew they were outclassed and were there for the paycheck. As far as I was concerned, that was no way to be. I intended for my stay in Arizona to be an opportunity to better myself.

Earl Weaver was managing the Baltimore Orioles rookies. The Orioles had the bases loaded and one out, and the batter hit a fly ball that the right fielder came in on. While he was waiting under it, I called the batter out, citing the infield-fly rule. When the outfielder dropped the ball, I still maintained that the batter was out. Earl came out to argue.

"You can't call that an infield fly," he said. "It was caught by an outfielder."

"No, he's out," I said. "The rule says an infield fly is any ball that can be caught with ease. It doesn't say who can catch it. It's a ball that can be handled with ease with runners at first and second or runners at first, second, and third."

Earl didn't believe me.

"I'll bet your goddamn ass that you're dead wrong," he said.

"You better talk to Joe DiMaggio," I said.

"What do you mean?"

"Mr. DiMaggio was the one who caused the change in the rule," I said, "because he would come in with that gun of an arm. He would call the infielder off, let the ball bounce once, catch it and gun it to second, and then the second baseman would throw to third and get the man there for a double play."

I told him, "The rule says an infield fly is any ball that can be caught with ease. It doesn't say who can catch it. It's a ball that can be handled with ease with runners on first and second or runners on first, second, and third. Read the rule book, Earl."

The next day Earl came over and was a man about it.

"By God, I have to apologize," he said sheepishly. "You were right. It can be called if an outfielder catches it."

From then on Earl and I had a lot of respect for each other, even though I never umpired another game managed by him.

Earl evidently wasn't the only person noticing how right I was about the rules.

At the end of the Instructional League season in Arizona a chubby little man walked over to my wife, who was sitting in the stands, and gave her his card. Joy thought he was old enough to be her grandfather.

"Your husband is too good to be in C ball," he said. "Tell him I can get him a better job."

He told her his name was Pants Rowland, a longtime baseball man. Rowland had managed the 1917 Chicago White Sox to a pennant and was fired the next year after a fight with owner Charlie Comiskey. His getting fired probably saved his reputation. He would have been the manager of the 1919 Black Sox had he not been fired. He then became a scout with the Chicago Cubs and then was an American League umpire for many years. In the mid-1940s Rowland became an executive with the Pacific Coast League. He was still with the league when he scouted me.

Not knowing anything about him, I told my wife, "Don't get too excited, dear. People promise a lot of things."

Within a week I received a telegram from Dewey Soriano, the president of the Triple-A Pacific Coast League, offering me a contract.

I was jumping from C ball over B ball, over A ball, over AA ball, all the way to Triple-A ball. It wasn't supposed to be done that way. But that was my reward for all the hard work.

CHAPTER 7

NOTICED IN PUERTO RICO

— 1 —

My year in the Pacific Coast League was uneventful. I can't remember one vicious argument or even a hiccup. A fellow by the name of Pat Orr was my crew chief. Pat had been in the league quite a while, and it didn't take me long to discover that his eyesight was failing. During the first games we worked he was umpiring at third base, and I noticed when a batter hit a line drive down the third-base line, Pat didn't turn to see if the ball was fair or foul. It was a sign he didn't see it. If I was the home-plate umpire, I would cover for him, making the call from behind home plate.

Pat sought to mentor me, which I appreciated greatly, but I didn't need all that much mentoring. I was thirty-one years old and more mature than most guys coming into the league. At least Pat didn't try to bury me, like others tried to do during my career. Pat was a fine, fine gentleman. I thought the world of him. I'd have done anything for him.

One of the other umpires in the Pacific Coast League was Emmett Ashford, the first African American umpire to make it to the big leagues. Emmett had worked in El Centro, California, my hometown, so I had known him quite a while. He had been over at our house and had dinner with our family. When he made it to the big leagues, *Life* magazine did a story on him in which he told the reporter that my dad had taught him everything he knew. I don't know where he got that idea. He saw my dad perhaps twice a year at most.

No one I can remember gave Emmett a hard time because he was black, except his umpiring partner Cece Carlucci, who umpired in the Pacific Coast League for many years. They were partners for twelve years, and no one knew it, but they hated each other. Cece was angry at Emmett because the NAACP lent Emmett a car, which he used to drive from town to town. He never once offered to give Cece a ride, so Cece had to pay for his own transportation out of his per diem. The NAACP gave Emmett the car in the hopes he would become the first one to make it in the major leagues—and he did. And Art Williams, the second African American to make it to the big leagues, came from Bakersfield.

— 2 —

By the time I was umpiring in the Pacific Coast League, I had learned a number of important lessons about the mechanics of umpiring that stood me in good stead all through my years in the major leagues.

I have five rules. They're simple, real easy, nothing to them. If you memorize them, I swear you'll be better off than a lot of umpires I've seen in my time.

First, when the ball comes in, listen for the ball to hit the glove. *Bam*. And if there are no runners on base, then count one thousand and one. Your mind will replay the pitch. If it's a pitch that surprises you and makes you suck wind, which shivers you, then you call out "Strike."

Second, if you're umpiring in the infield and a ball is hit to the outfield, you go running out there and set yourself. Don't watch it come down into the glove. Watch it until it gets to within thirty feet of the fielder and then leave the ball and watch his glove. You'll never miss that call again. When you run out there, your eyes are bouncing. If you don't stop and watch the glove, you won't see what happens correctly.

Third, on a ball hit down the line, a shot over the bag either down the first- or third-base line, remember this: If you watch the ball, and it's so close that you can't really tell—a really difficult call—then you call it a fair ball. Why? Because the batter beat the pitcher.

Fourth, you know how they say a tie goes to the runner? It's true, but it's not in the rule book. Here's what the rule book says: *The throw must beat the runner.* So yes, I guess you can say a tie goes to the runner, but make sure it's actually a tie before you call it that way.

Fifth, I often get asked, "Is the black part of the plate a strike?"

Hell, no. The black is strictly there for background. The plate is white, not black.

Finally (and I'll talk about this later in the book), you ought to go by Harvey's Rule of Thumb: Any time a player or manager gets personal, he's gone. You can tell me I made a horseshit call. Fine. That's your opinion of my call. But the second you walk up and say, "Harvey, you're horseshit," you're gone.

Let me tell you something else about this wonderful game of baseball. If you as the manager don't like my call on the base paths, you should be coming out. One of my compadres, umpire Nestor Chylak, didn't believe in arguments. He would tell managers, "If you come out, I'll bury you."

I don't approve of that. Every man has a right to come out and talk to me. Any time there was a close play, I just assumed someone would come and argue. If they didn't, I would say to myself, *You're an idiot. You should have come out and said something.*

So I expected it. And I was okay with it, so long as you didn't get up in my face. Then I'd say, "Back off or get out," and they would back off real quick.

I also learned a lot about positioning myself behind the plate.

Get yourself a stance that isn't debilitating, because you're going to be there all game long. Short umpires have it easier on their legs than tall umpires, because the tall umpires have to bend down.

One question: How close to the catcher should you stand?

One of the first things I learned as a young umpire was you don't have to crowd the catcher. In fact, *crowding the catcher is the worst thing you can do*. And when they start out, most umpires crowd the catcher. They get on the catcher's back and can't see the other side of the plate. In fact, you really can't see the strike zone at all. You think you can, but you can't. Believe it or not, when you back off, you are better able to see the ball coming through the strike zone.

I've backed umpires up as many as fifteen feet back and to the left or right to get them to see that what I'm saying is true. Usually I asked them to step three steps back and three steps to the right for a righty batter and three steps to the left for a lefty batter.

The young umpires think I'm crazy, but after the first pitch they're aware they can see the entire strike zone perfectly.

I also tell my students to stand with the right leg behind the left. That way, if the ball hits you in the mask, it knocks you back and the back leg softens the blow. I have recommended this ever since I saw Eric Gregg, who weighed more than three hundred pounds, take a foul ball on his chin. His feet were side by side, and when the ball hit him, he toppled over on his back like a big oak tree. I wouldn't want that to happen to anyone.

The last thing I would tell a young umpire: Control your temper. But as you will see throughout this book, for a lot of umpires this is extremely difficult to do.

— 3 —

My only beef about my year in the Pacific Coast League was that Joy and I were living in San Diego—San Diego had a team in the league—and I told league president Dewey Soriano that I was newly married and wanted to be able to see my wife during the season. That son of a bitch assigned me to umpire games in San Diego exactly once. I was sent to Hawaii six times, but even though Joy was working full-time for a title company, it was still too expensive for her to join me there. We were making $500 a month, and from that we had to pay rent, utilities, and transportation. In fact, Joy couldn't afford to drive the car to work and park it downtown, so she took the bus.

"We got to share the same ocean, and that was about it," was the way she put it.

At the end of the season I kept my trap shut and applied with the league to work in the Puerto Rican winter league.

"Is there any chance I can go?" I asked Soriano.

Apparently there was.

I was sitting at the dinner table at home in October when the phone rang.

"Meester Harvey?"

"Yes."

"Meester Gillees told me I call you. You come to Puerto Rico."

"Whoa, whoa," I said. "What are you talking about?"

"Don't you been told?"

"No," I said.

"I have Mr. Gillees give you a call."

And he hung up on me.

Who the hell is Mr. Gillees? I wondered. *And who was that calling me?*

The caller, it turned out, was the president of the Puerto Rican winter league.

Five minutes later the phone rang again.

"Doug Harvey?"

"Yes."

"This is Warren Giles."

Gillees. Giles. Oh, I thought to myself.

Warren Giles was the president of the National League.

"What can I do for you, sir?" I said.

"They are interested in having you umpire in the Puerto Rican League," Giles said.

"I'd love to do that, sir," I said.

"Do you want us to send you a ticket for you and your wife, or would you like to fly and then send us a bill?"

"No, send me the tickets," I said.

I didn't have the money to fly us to Puerto Rico and then get reimbursed.

There was only one problem with letting Mr. Giles buy the ticket for us: We went steerage class. We flew from San Diego to Fresno to Dallas to Miami to San Juan. It took us all day and all night, but when you're in love and newly married and happy to be with your wonderful wife, what difference does it make, really?

— 4 —

Because Joy was able to go with me, the entire winter season was like a honeymoon. We loved Puerto Rico. The league provided us with a little car and a cute little fifth-floor apartment. Sometimes the elevator didn't work, and we would have to drag our groceries up the stairs. I was assigned to the different cities and towns, and we got to tour the island a lot and had a wonderful time staying in little *casas*.

I was the only umpire in our crew who wasn't a major league umpire. I loved umpiring in Puerto Rico, even though the crowds could be rough. The fans were just that: fanatical. You knew as an umpire that you had to keep tight control, or a riot might break out at any moment.

In my short stay there I was involved in two riots. The first was the final championship game between rivals Santurce and Caguas at Hiram Bithorn Stadium in Santurce, which is a suburb of San Juan.

I had worked the plate the night before. My crewmates working the game were both local Puerto Rican umpires. The ballpark, Estadio Luis Rodríguez Olmo—named after the second Puerto Rican to play in the major leagues—was packed with fans of the Arecibo Lobos. Olmo, a legend in Puerto Rico, was managing the Lobos that day. The stadium had an odd shape: It was 545 feet down the right-field line and 490 feet down the left-field line. If you drew a straight line from foul pole to foul pole, you'd find that center field measured only about 204 feet.

Arecibo and Santurce were tied. Arecibo, batting in the bottom of the eighth, had runners at first and second base with two outs when an Arecibo batter hit a fly ball to center field. The runners on first and second, sure the ball was going to be a home run, went halfway and held, as the center fielder went back, tapping his glove as though he was going to catch it. He jumped, but the ball was over his head, and it hit the top of the center-field wall and bounced halfway back to second base.

A Santurce fielder picked up the ball and threw a dart into second. I was umpiring at first base and had run out to the outfield to see whether or not the ball was going to be caught. The umpire at third was supposed to cover second, but he was late getting there. The throw came to the second baseman, who slapped the runner with his glove. From where I stood I thought the runner was safe at second, but the third-base umpire, trailing the play, called him out. The runner from second base did not cross the plate until after the tag was made, and because the umpire called the runner at second out, the run does not score.

When the other umpire called the runner out, the Arecibo fans began to holler and scream and carry on something awful. Then Santurce scored in the top of the ninth, Arecibo went down meekly in the bottom without scoring a run, Santurce won the championship, and all hell broke loose.

The phalanx of Arecibo fans seated in the outfield, drunk and very angry, began tearing down the chain-link fencing, jumping over the five-foot-high fence and pouring onto the field. When I noticed this mayhem was building, I ran to grab the other two umpires in order to lead them to safety. At home plate one of the umpires was arguing with the Arecibo manager Olmo, and at second base the other umpire was arguing with a couple of the Arecibo players. I pulled on the arm of the second-base umpire, led him to home plate, and told both of them, "Fellas, grab my belt, and let's get out of here."

We were pushing against the crazed, out-of-control fans, trying to get off the field, when one fan came at us swinging a two-by-four slab of wood. He swung it overhand in an attempt to separate my head from my body. I threw up my arm and when he hit it, the two-by-four split, and with my arm in front of my head, I drove him to the ground and started pounding him.

Looking back, what I found most interesting about all of this was that I wasn't nervous or intimidated in the least. I was very calm. When you're young and in love and when you enjoy umpiring as much as I did, you just find it all very exciting.

Anyway, this guy with the two-by-four was down on the

ground moaning, and oh my God, those fans were furious, trying to tear my shirt off. I got up and started pushing my way past them, when from up above—as though it were coming from heaven—I could hear this voice command: "Get back. Get back."

The rowdies stopped what they were doing and stared.

God almighty, I thought. *He's here to save me.*

I looked up, and it wasn't God, but rather I was looking at the chin of big Frank Howard, an outfielder who, at six foot seven and 250 pounds, towered over me and the diminutive Puerto Ricans.

"Get back," he bellowed at the fans, as he led me and the other two umpires off the field and to relative safety. There wasn't another punch thrown.

We arrived at the dressing room, which didn't have a ceiling. From outside the stadium, fans were pelting the dressing room with rocks, and I could hear thwacks as the rocks hit the walls of the dressing room. The players also used the dressing room, and someone was letting the fans outside know when the players were entering, and they stopped throwing rocks so the players could dress and get the hell out of there.

"Harv, are you all right?" asked one of the Santurce players.

It was Bob Uecker, their catcher.

"My wife is in the stands, and she's pregnant," I said.

"I'll go find her," said Uecker, "and I'll take her out and send word back about where you can pick her up."

Uecker went and got her and dropped her off at a San Juan pizza joint. He got word back to me where she was waiting.

It was two and a half hours before the police could get a squad car to us and take me to my automobile so I could go and get Joy.

When I finally got to her, her eyes were as big as plates.

"My God," she said. "I was so afraid for you."

"Don't be afraid," I told her. "I was enjoying it."

— 5 —

Later, there was a similar but less dangerous riot during a championship game between San Juan and Santurce. San Juan and Santurce are like the Yankees and the Red Sox. Every game was like a war, and I was surprised when I was chosen to be the umpire behind the plate. I figured that Mel Steiner, who had been in the big leagues for five years, would do it, because I had worked the plate the game before. But I also wasn't surprised when he chose to work first base and make me umpire the plate again. Steiner would do that. Both Steiner and Paul Pryor were National League umpires, and I was a Pacific Coast umpire. There was nothing I could do but accept it.

When I arrived in our clubhouse before the game, Steiner

and Pryor saw I wasn't wearing my protective gear and wanted to know why.

"Because I didn't think I was working the plate," I said.

"Yes, you are," I was told.

Luckily, our hotel was only a block or so away, so I ran back and got my gear on. I didn't mind umpiring behind the plate at all, though I was quickly learning that a number of major league umpires couldn't stand the pressure and dreaded it. They would walk around in a daze for three days, just terrified because they knew that soon they'd be back there again. I looked forward to the challenge.

Toward the end of the game, the bases were loaded. San Juan went to bat trailing by a run. There was one out. A ball was hit to the shortstop, who made a nice play and threw to second, and the second baseman threw to first just as the runner was arriving. If the runner was safe, the game would be tied. All eyes turned toward Mel Steiner.

After the ball hit the first baseman's glove, Mel didn't say a word. He hooked his thumb in his belt and pointed. No one could tell from his actions whether the runner was safe or out. When Mel started to walk off the field, it became clearer that he had called the runner out. With Steiner's out call, San Juan had lost the game.

The manager of the San Juan team was Nap Reyes, who weighed about three hundred pounds. Reyes couldn't believe his runner at first was out, and he looked like an angry bull as he came thundering past me. Reyes and Steiner went at it as the crowd began a full-blown riot. I got about halfway to first when Reyes and Mel went to the ground and started rolling around. Now the fans were *really* going crazy.

There was a hearing at the San Juan racetrack that lasted two days. It was held there because the track had the only replay machine. We weren't allowed to go home until the hearing was over. In the end, San Juan had still lost, but Mel wasn't welcomed back to Puerto Rico the next year.

Mel was kind of a strange duck. We were umpiring a spring-training game in old Wrigley Field in Los Angeles. I was working the plate, Mel was at third. The bases were loaded. The batter swung and hit a ball that hit Mel right in the chest. As a result, the team at bat only scored one run.

After the game I said to him, "What were you thinking?"

"I had just invested some money in the stock market," he said, "and I was wondering how it was doing."

"Holy shit, Mel," I said, "you don't think about stocks when you're umpiring baseball."

"It's only spring training," he said. "What do I give a shit?"

I could only shake my head.

One highlight of my stay in Puerto Rico was getting to watch Roberto Clemente play in his home country. Clemente was God in Puerto Rico. He was a good man. The way he died was tragic. How many men would risk their lives flying food and supplies to victims of an earthquake?

— 6 —

We met a lot of interesting people in Puerto Rico. Sometimes it's really great to be poor, because you appreciate everything so much. When you get to do things that ordinarily you can't afford, they're always special.

New Year's Eve was special. We had wanted to go see the pianist and entertainer Victor Borge, but the tickets were something like $75, and we couldn't afford that. Joy was pregnant, and we were trying to save up enough to have a family. We had to pay the medical bills, because umpires in the minor leagues didn't have health insurance. Instead, we bought roman candles and went out and shot them over the San Juan wharf. They illuminated all the rats running around.

CHAPTER 8

HOOPS

— 1 —

For twenty-seven years, I refereed basketball. It's how I made money during the winter after the baseball season was over. I was as good a basketball official as I was an umpire. My brother Nolan and I were a team. Nolan just went into the San Diego Hall of Fame as a basketball official. I'm there for baseball. Nolan and I were probably the best refereeing crew in Southern California.

I started in high school. I can remember one game played at Hoover High School in San Diego. Hoover High was winning by quite a lot, and the other team was getting a little rough. In games like that, Nolan and I thought it best to just let the kids play, because the outcome wasn't in doubt.

Bob Warner, who was the coach at Hoover High, called time, and he said to me, "Doug, come on. They're fouling."

"Bob, I know," I said. "I've got control of it. Just tell your kids that if they get too rough, I'll call it. But if it's a slight foul, I'm not going to, because you're so far ahead. Let's get this game over with."

"Fine," he said.

That was my approach.

I can remember another game when I needed to take control in order to keep it fair. The game pitted Hoover High against rival Lincoln High School. In those days the schools were segregated; Hoover was all-white and Lincoln all-black. The game was at Lincoln, and few Hoover fans went. They were too afraid. I was one of the very few white faces in the game that night.

Early in the game I was standing on the end line holding the ball when one of the Lincoln students walked by me.

"If Hoover wins," he said, "I'll slit your throat."

I went over to the coach's bench, watching the kid the whole way. I told the guy in charge of security what he had said, and he raced and caught the kid as he headed to the boys' bathroom. He took him outside, and I don't know what happened to him.

But I could see that Hoover was being homered. The other referee, who was black, wasn't calling fouls on Lincoln, so I took charge of the whole ball game. Normally I'd never embarrass my partner, but he was playing favorites and it made me sick. I decided that the only way the game would be fair was if I stepped in.

Hoover won in the last seconds. The home-team fans weren't happy.

The security guard grabbed me and started to lead me out of the gym, when I became concerned for my partner. Lincoln had lost, and I feared that their fans might take it out on him. I raced over to where he was, only to see him laughing and joking and having a ball with the Lincoln fans.

I hated to see something like that, but that's the way it was back then.

I was also hired as a referee for the games played by California Western University, a school in San Diego. The athletic director, whose name I no longer can remember and who went on to become a general manager in the NBA, hired me.

I refereed the California Western games, and halfway through the season I got a call from the assignment secretary, informing me that the California Western coach and AD no longer wanted me to referee their games. The problem, as I saw it, was that he wanted the referees to be homers who gave his team an advantage, and I refused to do that.

"He says you're too strict and you don't give him any breaks," said the assignment secretary.

"That's his fucking problem, not mine," I said. "I'm not worried. Can you get me ball games for those days?"

"Hell yes," he said. "I'll get you a game anytime."

That night he assigned me to a junior-college game. I went and worked it and afterward came home. My phone rang. It was almost midnight. The assignment secretary was calling about that night's Cal Western game.

"Doug, they almost had a riot in Long Beach," he said. "This new referee walked out onto the court like he was the King of Prussia and told everybody, 'I'll run this game, and I don't want anybody fucking with me.' And it wasn't long before the two teams got into a fistfight, and they almost had a riot. Is there any chance you can go back there and pick his game up tomorrow?"

"Yeah," I said. "Why the hell not?"

In refereeing, as it is with umpiring, stature is everything. You have to have a presence on the court. You have to make the coaches and players respect you. You do it by getting the calls right and knowing the rules. You also get it by allowing the coaches to have a say without letting them be disrespectful. Your job is to control the game. I could do that.

The next night, I walked out onto the court. I called the coaches and team captains for a meeting.

"Gentlemen, you know me from before," I said. "You either play basketball or I'm going to dump you. I want you to know that in advance. I'm not going to call technical fouls. You get out of line, and I'm going to dump the troublemakers. Screw around, and I'm going to dump you.

"Now you go back and tell your people, fuck with me, and I'll fuck ya."

That's the way I did it.

I was a great basketball official.

— 2 —

One night at the end of the 1961 baseball season I received a call from Abe Saperstein, who owned the Harlem Globetrotters. The Globetrotters were coming to San Diego, and I was hired to officiate their game against the Washington Generals, the patsy team they beat almost every night. After it was over, Saperstein said to me, "You know how to do it. How would you like to go on the road with us?"

I didn't want to go on the road. I was on the road enough during the baseball season. It's hard enough being away from your family for up to ten weeks at a time during the summer. Over a seven-month season, I averaged only nine nights at home sleeping in my own bed. It wasn't until the league put a team in San Diego in 1969 that I got home more often.

My wife kept a picture of me by the phone so that when I called, the boys could see my face. If I was on the road and one of the boys got in trouble, all their mother had to do was tell them, "I'm putting your father on the phone."

Then I'd straighten them out real quick, saying, "Listen, you, you better do what your mother tells you to do—or else."

It scared them half to death, but it worked every time.

Saperstein must have liked my work refereeing the Globetrotter game, because he called me when he started a new basketball league called the ABL, the American Basketball League. The league featured, for the first time, the three-point goal.

Abe Saperstein—who was from Chicago, not Harlem—said to me, "I need referees, Doug. Can you be in Long Beach in two days and work three straight days? Can you do it for me?"

"Yes, sir, I can do that," I said. "What about the rules?"

"I'll have the rules sent to you," he said.

In two days? I thought. *Not very organized.*

I didn't travel; rather I refereed games in Long Beach, Los Angeles, and Anaheim.

The Los Angeles Chiefs were owned by a man by the name of Kim. In L.A., we finished a game in which the Chiefs lost. After I stopped and signed the score book, I came around a corner and I could hear this guy Kim berating Paddy Denoy, one of the other officials.

I walked into the officials' clubhouse, and I could see Kim yelling at him.

"What are you doing in here?" I asked Kim.

"I'm Kim, the owner of the ball club," he said.

"I don't give a goddamn who you are," I told him. "Get out of here."

"I'll leave when I'm ready to leave," he said.

"You'll leave now," I told him.

When he just stood there, I walked over, picked him up under one arm, and carried him a good twenty yards from our dressing room to the door.

After the game my wife asked me, "Doug, what happened?"

She was standing outside our dressing room, waiting for me.

"This guy came in, so I carried him and put him outside the door and closed it," I said.

"*Put* him outside?" she said. "He flew outside. You threw him ten feet."

I have no recollection of any of it.

They wanted me to work the play-offs, but I couldn't do it because I had to get back to baseball. The ABL folded after two years of play. The winner the second year was the Cleveland Pipers, owned by a young George Steinbrenner, who later became the owner of the New York Yankees. Steinbrenner never left Cleveland, so I never saw him in action. But I understand he constantly undermined his coach, the great John McLendon, and later replaced him with Bill Sharman because he wanted someone more famous. Steinbrenner also was thrown out of a number of games for going out onto the court and arguing with the referees. I'm sorry I didn't get to see that.

— 3 —

When the ABL folded after only two seasons, I went back to refereeing college ball. I was getting paid $35 a game to referee Pac-8 basketball, a league that included UCLA, USC, and the University of California.

I was refereeing a game with UCLA and was running up the court, and I could see UCLA coach John Wooden standing there tapping his left hand with the program that he always carried. He was tapping his left hand, *tap, tap, tap, tap*. That meant: *I'm feeling annoyed.* I could read signals.

I went down the court and came back, and he was still *tap, tap, tap, tap*ping.

"They're all over Walton," Wooden said to me. Walton was UCLA's star center Bill Walton.

"Okay, John. I'll watch it," I said.

I went up the court as UCLA went on offense, and I watched Walton to see what was going on. He wasn't getting hammered any more than he was hammering them. It's a rough game. We went down the other end of the court and came back, and I could see Coach Wooden *tap, tap, tap, tap*ping hard, and he said to me, "Harvey, they're all over Walton."

Oh, this is too much, I thought to myself, and I blew my whistle. Wooden was putting the heat on me to gain an edge. I stopped the game to let everyone know what he was doing.

I pointed at him the same way I would point at a high school kid not to do something.

"Coach Wooden, I heard you," I said. "I don't need to be reminded. Now back off, or we're going to get technical."

I blew my whistle and handed the ball to the player, then ran down the court, and that was the last thing he said to me that evening.

That was the way I refereed. For the rest of the game Wooden kept tapping, but I didn't mind it. What I didn't want him doing was hammering me vocally. I let him know I was a little bit perturbed.

I loved refereeing in the Pac-8. I refereed a game at the University of California at Berkeley. They were playing the University of Nebraska, and Pete Newell was the Cal coach.

Cal had a 15-point lead, and, one by one, Newell took out his starters. *Bim bam boom*, there were a couple of fouls, and Nebraska hit some shots, and as the lead began to disappear he put his starters back in.

One of his players grabbed the ball and dunked it. Back then it was against the rules to dunk. Kareem Abdul-Jabbar (then called Lew Alcindor) had come into the league, and the rule was passed to try to slow him down. Other players had broken backboards dunking, so the other rationale was to cut down on busted backboards.

The Cal player had dunked, and so I waved off the points. It was one of the reasons Cal lost the game.

After the game I had to sign the score book. The other referee headed for the dressing room. When I walked in there, I could see Newell screaming at him. He was hollering that we had fucked up the game, that we never should have called interference and waved off the basket, and we should have done this, shouldn't have done that . . . and he was screaming.

I tapped Newell on the shoulder.

"Coach," I said, "you're in the wrong dressing room."

"I'll tell you where the fuck I can be," he said. "I'm the coach here, and I'm also the athletic director."

My Scotch-Indian blood began to boil.

"You better walk through that fucking door," I said, "or I'm going to throw you through it. And you have one second."

Newell was chickenshit to fight me. He took a step toward me and said, "I'll get your job."

And he ran out.

I was going to say to him, "If you can get my job, I don't want it," but it turned out that he *did* get my job. Pete Newell was a big dog. He had taken California to a national championship, led by Darrell Imhoff, who later went to the New York Knicks and was pretty much a failure. One reason Imhoff failed as a pro was that he had been allowed to push the college centers around and score points. In the pros he went up against Wilt Chamberlain and Bill Russell, and he didn't stand a chance.

They even took my job in a chickenshit way. They sent me a note saying, *Your services are no longer needed*. Which I thought was chickenshit. If you're going to fire someone, fire him to his face.

— 4 —

The invitation to referee in the American Basketball Association came with a phone call.

"Can you be in Dallas tomorrow night?" I was asked.

"I could be," I said, "but I don't know why I would want to."

"Excuse me," the caller said, "but this is George Mikan. We have just formed a new basketball league, and we have everything all set except the officials. I was told you're a very good referee, and we need you."

George Mikan was one of the legends of the game. As a center with the Minnesota Lakers in the late forties to mid-fifties, he was six foot ten, 250 pounds of muscle, and so overpowering that the league introduced the shot clock and widened the foul lanes to keep him from dominating. I felt honored when I heard it was Mr. Mikan calling me.

"The ABA will pay you seventy-five dollars a game plus expenses," he said. Since the colleges were only paying $35 a game, I accepted, even though it meant having to go back on the road.

"Sign me up," I said. "Get me a schedule and get me a rule book. I'll be there."

The next morning I got on an airplane and flew to Dallas.

That night I met with the coaches and captains at center court before the game. I gave my usual pregame talk.

"If you play decent ball," I said, "we won't have any problems."

"Hey, we know what we're doing," said Cliff Hagan, the Dallas Chaparrals' player-coach. He had been a college all-American at Kentucky and a big star in the NBA.

"I don't need this shit," I told him, "and I'm going to tell you right now, if you fuck around, I'm going to stick it up your ass. Let's go to work."

The game began, and I hit Hagan with two technical fouls and threw him out of the game during the first two minutes. And every time I refereed Hagan's games, he gave me trouble.

The ABA sent me all over the country to referee. It was a terrible time for Joy and me. She added it up, and that year I was home for a total of thirteen days. But that's how I made enough money to pay my bills and live.

I even had to spend New Year's on the road. One time I ran across some of the NBA referees, and they blanched when they learned of my schedule. All they paid was $75 a game, which was still more than I could make in college ball. The problem was I couldn't make that $75 seven days a week. As a result, I was constantly on the go.

I can remember one game in Indianapolis. We played in an older stadium, and the floor was slippery because the basketball court was laid over ice. That evening I called six technical fouls against the home-team Pacers. I ejected the coach and also the general manager. Hell, they were mouthing off, wanting us to call different things. The general manager should not have been on the bench.

"You'll have to leave," I told him.

"Fuck you, I'm not going," he said.

I unloaded him.

The Pacers still won the game by 12 points.

The ABA was interesting because it allowed several players who had been caught up in the college point-shaving scandals of the early 1960s to play in the league. One of them was Connie Hawkins, who supposedly had taken $75 from a gambler when he was a freshman at the University of Iowa. Connie, who played high school ball in Brooklyn, was barred from finishing his college career and also from playing in the NBA. He later sued the NBA and won millions of dollars.

I loved Connie. He was a sweetheart. During a game he came by and said to me, "Harvey, this guy is really roughing me up." The player who was guarding him and working him over with his elbows had played at California Western. I had refereed his college games and knew him to be a good kid, but on this night he was working Connie over pretty good. I could see blood on Connie's face.

"Connie, what shall we do?" I asked.

"If you'll turn your head two times," Connie said, "I can straighten him out."

The next time Connie went down the court on offense I turned my head, but at the same time was looking out of the side of my face, and I could see Connie standing under the basket, staring at the rafters. The kid who was guarding him slid over in front of him, and he also looked up, and when he did, Connie nailed him with his elbow like you wouldn't believe. *Wham*, he smacked him across the face. The blood flowed, I stopped the game, and the kid had to go to the bench for treatment.

The kid came running onto the court.

"How come you let that happen?" he asked me.

"Because you've been nailing him all day long," I said. "If you don't stop it, I'm going to let him do it again."

I went over and told Connie, "No more."

"No more, Harv," Connie said.

That's the man he was. I loved Connie.

One of the other players caught up in the college gambling scandal was Alex Groza, the star center of the University of Kentucky. Groza too was barred from playing in the NBA, and like Connie, Groza was a terrific fellow.

The first game I had him, I gave my usual center-court professional talk, which was: "Boys, if you want to mess around, I'll stick it to you. If you want to play basketball, I'll let you play. It's that simple. Now, do what you want."

Groza said to me, "You'll have no trouble from me."

In one of the games, the fellow guarding Groza kept elbowing him, and Groza said to him, "Don't do that." He kept it up, and like Connie, Alex said to me, "Can you turn your head for a few minutes?"

I did, and Alex took care of him. These were the true professionals.

— 5 —

In the middle of the season I got a call from the NBA. The head of referees called me. They knew I was the best referee the ABA had, and they were trying to bust up the league.

"We want you to come to the NBA," he said.

"I have a job," I said. "I agreed to referee the ABA's games."

"We'll give you sixty thousand dollars a year."

That was a lot of money, but I didn't think twice.

"No," I said. I had agreed to referee in the ABA, and I wasn't about to go back on my word.

I got one more call.

"This is the last time I'm going to ask you. And I know you don't even have a contract."

He had done his homework. It was true I hadn't signed a contract. I hadn't even shaken the man's hand, but I had agreed to referee for the season. I again told him no.

"I've given my word, and my word is my bond," I told him. "I'm not going to break it, not for all the money in the world. If you want to call me for next season, I'll do it."

He never called again.

In 1976 the Pacers—along with the Denver Nuggets, New York Nets, and San Antonio Spurs—moved to the NBA as the two leagues merged.

I probably should have taken the NBA job, because it wasn't long after I turned them down that I resigned as an ABA referee.

George Mikan, the ABA commissioner, had hired his brother to be head of officials, and I thought he was doing a good job. Even though the ABA had a very fine group of referees, including former NBA refs Norm Drucker, Earl Strom, John Vanak, Joe Gushue, and Jack Madden, complaints by coaches and general managers about the officiating were rampant. They would get on the phone to the main office and bitch and moan about the officiating. Midway through the season, George Mikan, hearing all the complaints about what a terrible job his brother was doing, fired him, which I thought was wrong and terribly unfair.

As soon as I heard about it, I quit.

I was in the airport heading to my last game when I ran into Connie Hawkins, who was a sweetheart.

"Where are you going, Harv?" he wanted to know.

I told him I was flying to work my last game and that I was going to quit at the end of the week.

"Harvey, don't quit," he pleaded. "You're the best official in the league. Don't quit."

"Connie," I said, "the commissioner screwed some of my partners, and I don't want to work for him anymore."

"Let me tell you something," he said. "We're going to miss you."

Hearing that from Connie meant a lot to me.

CHAPTER 9

AL BARLICK'S WHIPPING BOY

— 1 —

After the Puerto Rican winter league season was over, I was asked by Fred Fleig, the head of National League officials, to meet in Salt Lake City, where I was umpiring a Pacific Coast League preseason game. Fleig informed me that he had selected me to become an umpire in the National League and that in a few days I'd be going to Florida to work spring-training games. He said that Pedro Vázquez, the president of the Puerto Rican winter league, had told him, "We've been playing baseball down here for eighty years, and Doug Harvey's the best umpire I ever saw."

"I don't want you to tell anybody," Fleig said. "Only your wife."

I flew with my umpiring crew to Seattle, site of the main office of the Pacific Coast League. Seattle was where the umpires stopped to get their mail. The three of us approached the secretary's desk, and in front of the others she said, "Congratulations, Mr. Harvey. I understand you're going to spring training with the National League."

I stood there red-faced with the two other members of my crew. I had known about this for about a week, and I hadn't told them a thing about it. And they were pissed at me.

"Goddamn, you're going to major league spring training, and you're not good enough to tell your partners?" said Cece Carlucci.

All I could do was apologize for not telling him.

Carlucci worked the plate that afternoon, and the final batter of the game popped out. I watched the ball come down, saw the fielder catch it, turned around, and suddenly heard someone yell, "Look out!"

Carlucci, who was so angry that I was going to the major leagues and not he, had thrown his mask about thirty feet in the air into the infield. He could have hurt someone. But that was how angry and hurt he was. Cece never did make it to the majors himself.

I reached the majors faster than anyone else ever has. I had gone from Class C to the National League in just four years—all without my going to umpire school. Fleig assigned me to be part of the crew of veteran umpire Al Barlick.

— 2 —

When I stepped onto the field at Dodger Stadium opening day on April 10, 1962—the first regular-season game ever played there—the size of the place and sold-out crowd amazed me. I was just a farm kid from the Imperial Valley.

"What do you think of this joint?" Al asked me between innings.

"It looks like it could hold a lot of hay," I said.

Al laughed like hell and must've told the story a thousand times.

From the beginning I could see why he was called the King.

Al had a booming voice, and at the inaugural game at Chavez Ravine, I experienced him for the first time with his game face on. The ballpark was jammed. He was behind the plate. The pitcher threw the first pitch of the ball game, and Al raised his arm up to signal it was a strike. He bellowed a booming call of *"Stt-teeeeeeeeeeeeeeeek."* You should have seen the people stand up and cheer. They had never heard a voice like that in L.A. before. He shook the whole stadium. They loved him.

Al had no fear of anyone. If someone hollered from the bench, he would turn, walk eight to ten steps toward the bench, and he'd turn that voice loose.

"One more word from you assholes . . ."

It was enough to shut them up.

Of course, it wasn't fun when he turned his venom on me.

Barlick was a rough, tough Irishman who had been a long-time umpire in the league. His father had been a coal miner, and Al had been one too. Al had dropped out of high school his junior year to help support his family. He escaped the mines when he was hired to umpire in the minor leagues in his hometown of Springfield, Illinois. In 1940, he was hired by the major leagues as a replacement for the great Bill Klem. Al was twenty-five years old, one of the youngest umpires ever to work in the major leagues. He was from the Midwest and didn't trust anyone. You had to prove yourself before he would even consider talking to you. Once you proved yourself, he might not like you, but he'd respect you. Earning that respect wasn't easy.

When I arrived after spring training to join his crew, I could quickly see that Barlick was mad to the gunnels. We never seemed to have a nice word to say to each other, though I have to say that he was one of the greatest umpires in the history of the game. But because he went out of his way to torment me, I experienced two of the worst years of my life.

The two other umpires in our crew, Shag Crawford and Ed Vargo, tried to shield me from Al's tirades, seeking to make my life a little more bearable. Shag Crawford adopted me. If anyone was a man's man, it had to be Shag Crawford. I can't say enough about him.

But not even they could protect me from Al, who wasn't called the King for nothing. I worked under him for two full years, fully realizing how much Barlick resented me but never knowing why. He tried to drive me out of baseball, and I simply refused to leave.

It took all my skill and honor to keep him from running me out of the league. I just refused to give in to him.

I wanted so badly to tell someone what he was doing, but who was I going to tell? Fred Fleig was in charge of the umpires and he had hired me. I had too much pride to go see Fred about this. I also told myself, *If you can't handle your job between umpires, how the hell are you going to settle anything on the field?*

— 3 —

I was working with Al, Shag Crawford, and Ed Vargo, and after ball games we would drink too much. I was not, and am not, a good drinker.

Early in the season our crew had to get up before sunrise so we could catch a flight from Houston to Pittsburgh, and I showed up perhaps five minutes late. In front of the other members of the crew, Al ripped into me. He called me every son of a bitch in the world. I swallowed hard. I wanted to slug him, but didn't dare.

Since that incident I always had trouble sleeping on getaway days when we had to catch a plane. I was so afraid I would come down late and be the target of Al Barlick's wrath that I would lie awake all night for fear the alarm clock wouldn't ring. Finally I began taking a light sleeping pill so I could get some sleep.

Al could be underhanded. I remember a doubleheader in Houston my first year. The expansion Colt .45's, as they were known then, were playing Milwaukee in the old ballpark in Houston. The dressing room was a tin shed, hot and miserable. The Braves were at one end and we were at the other. Barlick was working first base and I was working home. During the game Henry Aaron asked about a pitch, and I told him it was a good pitch.

Aaron eventually walked. Later, between games, Barlick said to me, "Henry Aaron said you told him you blew the pitch, that you missed it."

"You're full of shit," I said.

"I'm not," Barlick said.

Between games of the doubleheader, I walked over to Henry.

"May I ask you a question, Henry?" I asked.

"Sure, go ahead," he said.

"Barlick told me that you told him I missed a pitch. Is that true?"

"No, that's not true," he said.

"Can you come over and tell Mr. Barlick?"

"No way," Aaron said. "I'm not getting myself into that kind of trouble."

"I understand," I said. "Thanks."

I walked back to Barlick.

"You're a fucking liar," I said. "I don't know what this is, but you have one hell of a problem going. Are you trying to blow me out of this league? Because you're not going to do it."

Barlick didn't talk to me for a week after that. That's how serious it got.

— 4 —

As miserable as he made my days, at night after games I was often the only one keeping Barlick company at the bar. For a while it had been Ed Vargo who drank with him, but Ed started excusing himself all the time and going upstairs to his room, and finally Al asked him what the hell was going on, because Ed was his bobo and drinking buddy. It turned out Ed was falling in love with his future wife, Betty. She worked for TWA out of San Francisco, and Ed was going up to his room every night to call her.

One night Barlick and I were sitting in the Sheraton Hotel bar in New York, and he exploded.

"The goddamn young umpires don't know they should be drinking with the King," he said.

Al and I would start with beers at the ballpark after the game, and then we'd drink at the hotel bar. Al would bemoan the fact that there were no umpires who brought credit to the game, and I'd sit and listen to this, and then we'd order stingers, his choice of obliteration. What I had to learn early was to stop drinking stingers with Al Barlick. My wife told me later in life that the way I was starting out my first year, she was sure I was going to become an alcoholic. At the same time, she had fears her dad would become one too—and those did prove to be true. It took me a while to see that in time I was going to be in trouble, because I never woke with a headache after drinking. So for me there was no fear of it.

Al was a heavy drinker, and the more he drank, the more abusive he'd become. I really didn't want to sit with him, but I was the new kid, and so I did it out of duty. By the end of the evening, we'd end up bad-mouthing each other. A couple of times, he wanted to fight me.

"I'll whip your ass right now," he'd tell me.

I finally called his bluff and challenged him to fight.

"Al, let me tell you something," I said. "You get sober, and I'll get sober, and I'll take you any time you want. In the morning, I'll meet you in the lobby at nine o'clock. We'll find a place and we'll fight."

This happened twice. I'd come down in the morning, but Al wouldn't show up. Because of my farming background, I've never been one to sleep very much at all, especially past sunup. If the sun was in the sky and I wasn't on that tractor, I was a dead man. I preferred to get up with a short night of sleep and take a walk, come back, and take a nap in the afternoon.

I had a daily routine. I'd get out of bed early, go right down to breakfast, and then no matter what city I happened to be in I'd immediately go out and walk for an hour. I'd stop and bullshit with people I'd gotten to know over the years, then pick up two newspapers, *USA Today* and the local paper. Then I'd take off for my second walk of the day for about an hour or so. I'd come back to the hotel at about four-thirty and then I'd have my evening meal. I'd go upstairs at about five o'clock and then rest for an hour. If I couldn't sleep, I'd put my arms by my side and lie perfectly still. Then I'd go to the ballpark.

That's what I did every day.

I've always cursed the day Fred Fleig assigned me to Al Barlick, but then when I got older I realized how much I had learned from him. Al was a tough taskmaster. One time I was umpiring at third base. The Cardinals were in Los Angeles, and Cards' third baseman, Ken Boyer, turned to me and said something funny, and I laughed out loud. Across from first base, where Al was, came this booming voice. He screamed across at me, "What the fuck are you smiling at?"

Nothing was going on, and from the first twenty rows of spectators and in both dugouts, everyone turned and looked at me. I was never so embarrassed in my life.

Though I hated him, Al Barlick taught me so much about my craft, and I shall forever be indebted to him for it. Al was old-school. He had a fear of nobody. He hollered and screamed. And he taught me an important lesson: *If you make a call, hang with it.* And that's the way I umpired.

Al taught me that to get the respect you needed to command as a great umpire, you had to be creative.

When Leo Durocher was a coach for Walter Alston on the Dodgers, Leo would come out of the dugout, holler something obscene at us, and get ejected about the sixth inning. Then we realized that five minutes after Leo left, a little, cute tootsie sitting in the box seats wearing a Dodger jacket also left. We asked a few questions and learned that yeah, she was Durocher's honey.

Not very long after we learned this, Leo hollered something at us, and Al Barlick walked over and told him, "Let me tell you something, Leo. I have to work here, and you're going to stay as well. You're not leaving. We've had all we're going to take of you walking out with your honey. So sit down and shut up."

Al called us together and said, "We're not to eject him."

Later Durocher managed the Cubs, and for the first year and a half he sat on the bench and kept his mouth shut. By the middle of the second season he saw he had some players—Ernie Banks, Billy Williams, Ron Santo, Fergie Jenkins—and it was then that he started running his mouth. I tossed Leo a couple of times. He was fun to toss. He'd come out and put on a big show.

"Get the hell away from me," I'd tell him. "Get out of my face."

I didn't need his crap.

Al also taught me practical lessons to follow away from the diamond as well.

"Don't ever take a drink from a ballplayer, Harv," he said. "Don't do anything with ballplayers."

I paid close attention to what he had to say, though I must say I did it with clenched teeth. What drove me every year those first few years was my determination to be a better umpire than Al Barlick.

— 5 —

I hated him—until I understood where his enmity came from. I didn't know any of this until a half dozen years later, when umpire Tony Venzon and I were having dinner at Johnny's Café and Steakhouse in Chicago, and the topic of conversation got around to Barlick.

Venzon had fought in World War II. He was part of a large group of American soldiers on reconnaissance in the woods. The commander sent him back to his jeep to get some papers he had forgotten. While he was away, the group was surrounded and captured by the Germans.

When Tony returned he saw all these American soldiers lying down. He thought they were kidding. But then when he walked over and saw all the blood, he realized the Germans had lined them all up and shot them. They were all dead.

Venzon was a fine umpire and a good friend.

"I could never understand why Al treated me the way he did," I said over dinner.

"Don't you know?" Venzon said.

"No, I don't."

He then proceeded to explain it to me.

"When you came to spring training in 1962," Tony said, "Al Barlick told everyone that Billy Williams was going to be the next umpire coming into the National League. The head of officials was Fred Fleig, and Fred went against the King's orders. He hired you instead."

The King had wanted Billy Williams, who had been on option to the National League for several years, and Al thought he should have been the next one to be brought up.

"Fleig said, 'No, I'm taking Harvey.'"

Barlick was called the King of Umpires, and Fleig had crossed him and chosen me instead. And then Fleig assigned me to Barlick's crew. And Al did everything he could to drive me out of the league.

That was the story behind it.

When Al retired in 1971, he called me on the phone. I was in a St. Louis hotel.

"Harvey," he said, "I'm at home, and I just want you to know all the problems we had, fifty percent of it was my fault. And I apologize to you and hope you will forgive me for having realized too late that you're a great umpire."

I was flabbergasted.

"Al, it's all water over the dam," I told him. "I forgave you many years ago."

I wasn't a man to hold a grudge. It's part of the reason I was a good umpire, though I have to wonder why Fleig assigned me to Barlick's crew. It confounds me to this day. What was Fred thinking?

Al also said to me, "Harvey, you're going to the Hall of Fame one day, and when you get there, I'll be with you."

Unfortunately, Al didn't live to see me get in. He passed away in 1995 at the age of eighty, and I wasn't inducted until 2010. Had he been alive, he'd have certainly been with me.

— 6 —

In addition to never socializing with ballplayers, managers, or coaches, I also made it a practice never to accept a drink from a team president, a general manager, or even someone from the league or commissioner's office. I felt it wasn't my job—but more to the point, I felt it wasn't right. My job was to be neutral, and I never wanted to put myself in a position where I might be accused of favoritism because I had accepted something—anything—from a ballplayer or a team official.

One night fellow umpire Jocko Conlan and I were in a bar in Milwaukee after a ball game having a beer, and a guy came over to my bar stool and bumped me. I turned around, and it was Dodger pitcher Sandy Koufax.

"Harv, you want a cigar?" Sandy asked.

"No, thanks," I said. "I don't accept gifts from ballplayers."

"Okay," he said, and he left me and walked over to a table with a group of Dodger ballplayers.

That taught me a lesson. I never again sat on a stool at a bar. I always went to a table, because no one can invite himself to a table.

When Sandy left the bar, he absentmindedly left his silver cigarette lighter in front of me. I picked it up and carried it around for two months before I could return it to him. Before a game at Dodger Stadium I caught him coming off an elevator heading for the Dodger dressing room and gave it back to him.

"Hey, Sandy," I said. "Here. I don't want your lighter. I don't want anything of yours."

I never wanted a player to think he got something special from me. I figured he was entitled to only one thing from me, and that was a fair strike zone.

I was working the '92 All-Star Game in San Diego, and President George H. W. Bush was going to throw out the first ball. They needed a place to hide him before the game, and so they asked if he could hang out with us in the umpires' dressing room. He came in with all his security people and it was crowded as hell. There was a knock on the door.

"Someone important wants to see you," the clubhouse man said to me.

"Mr. President," I asked, "I've got to ask you a favor. Could you get rid of your security people? There's someone outside I really want you to meet, and we've got too big a crowd in here."

"Just stay outside," the president told his security people. "Who the hell's going to come in here?"

I went outside and brought in Ted Williams. Ted and the president started talking fishing, and after a while I said, "Gentlemen, it's about time for you to head out there, and I have to get ready so I can work home plate."

Before Ted walked out, he said to me, "Harvey, I have to ask you something. They say they consider you the epitome of umpires. Let me ask you: What's your strike zone?"

"Ted," I said, "my strike zone starts at the front of home plate; it's from the knee to the breastbone, where it comes together according to how the man crouches. And if you're standing back in the box, the ball will pass you right there. That's why they always said that Doug Harvey has a terrible strike zone, because that's where the strike zone is."

"Is that right?" said Ted.

"Yes," I said.

"Shit," said Ted, "you'd have made a .320 hitter out of me."

And he left.

— 7 —

That first year on our first trip to Philadelphia I ran into Al Widmar, the scout from Philadelphia who told me I'd never make it to the big leagues because I had gray hair and chewed tobacco. Widmar, then the pitching coach of the Phillies, was sitting in the dugout.

I had the plate that day, and moments before the game Al was minding his own business when I walked over and put my foot on the first step.

"I'm here, partner, and I'm going to be here for a while," I told him.

Then I spit tobacco juice at his shoes and walked away.

— 8 —

When I came to the National League I thought I was the best base umpire there was. But I still had a lot to learn about the art of umpiring. Especially behind the plate. Early in my rookie year I learned an important lesson.

I even remember the date: It was May 11, 1962. The Dodgers and Cardinals were playing in the bottom of the second, the Cardinals batting, the Dodgers up 1–0. Stan Williams was pitching for the Dodgers. They called Stan "Big Daddy." He was six foot five and every bit of 230 pounds. The Cardinals' batter stepped in. The count was one ball and two strikes.

A fastball came in like two others before it. When it was about twenty feet out, I threw up my hand and yelled out "*Hrrrriiiiik-kkke*!" Then the ball cut six inches like nothing I'd ever seen. The pitch crossed the plate outside the strike zone. What could I do? I couldn't change the call. I'd already called strike three. It was the third out. The Dodgers trotted off the field.

The batter, waiting for someone to bring him his glove, turned his back to me. I figured I was in a shithouse of trouble. I was sure he was going to unload on me and get the crowd on my ass. But he never turned to face me. Over his shoulder he calmly said, "Young fella, I don't know what league you came from, but home plate is seventeen inches wide, same as it is here. If you want to stay up here, wait until the ball crosses the plate before you call it."

The batter was Stan Musial.

From then on, I never called a pitch until after it hit the catcher's mitt. That's the timing you try to set, and you do it beginning with the very first pitch of the ball game. The pitcher throws, the ball hits the catcher's glove, and you count to yourself "one thousand one," and during that time you try to see the pitch again in your mind's eye, and then you make the call. In a way you're seeing the pitch twice. But you must wait until a second or even two after the ball hits the glove to make the call. The one exception to this rule is if there's a runner on first base, in which case you have to make the call sooner. If the runner runs, the catcher has to know early whether it's a ball or a strike so he can decide whether or not to throw to second.

— 9 —

Another of the good guys was Milwaukee Braves catcher Del Crandall. It was early in my first season and I had the plate. Warren Spahn was pitching and Crandall was catching. Warren threw the first pitch of the game, and I said, "Ball."

Warren, who was the winningest left-hander of all time, walked down from the mound and said, "What?"

"The man said *ball,*" said Crandall.

"Jesus Christ, I can't throw a better pitch than that," said Spahn.

"I guess you're in a heap of trouble," Crandall said.

Spahn turned around and walked back up onto the mound, and he kept his mouth shut the rest of the day. Crandall was a very fair person. Spahn, like most pitchers, just wanted anything close he could get, and guys like him liked to test the new umpires. Yeah, they would test you badly. That first year they would test me every minute of the day.

— 10 —

With every game I learned something. The most difficult manager I ever had to face was Freddie Hutchinson of the Cincinnati Reds. Back in those days, Hutchinson was a real beauty.

He was on me the very first series I worked in the major leagues in 1962.

By the third game of the season-opening series between the Reds and the Dodgers at Dodger Stadium, I had rotated to first base. On a close play at first, Gordy Coleman, the Reds first baseman, pulled his foot from the bag an instant before the runner arrived. I called him safe. Fred came out and started in, ranting and raving.

"What the fuck's going on?" he demanded to know. He could no more hold a conversation without cursing than he could flap his arms and fly.

This is where the creativity I learned from Al Barlick came in handy.

"Didn't you get the notice?" I said.

"What notice?" he asked, a little puzzled.

"The one that said this year we're going to concentrate really hard on keeping the first baseman's foot on the bag," I said. "There'll be no cheating."

"Well, I'll be a son of a bitch. This guy's here three days and he's gonna change the whole goddamned way of umpiring," he muttered as he left the field. Fred, a former pitcher, was about six foot four, and he was six foot four of hell on umpires—until I stood up to him one day. And when I did that, I could see he had a lot more respect for me. That was something I had to learn.

It happened on a day when I was working the plate in another Reds–Dodgers game. Hutchinson was managing, Maury Wills was the first batter for the Dodgers, and Bob Purkey was pitching for the Reds. The first pitch came in and I called it a ball. I could hear a voice coming from the dugout. It was Fred.

"Well, you're oh-for-one," he yelled out.

The next pitch was fouled off, and Fred yelled, "Great, now you're one-for-two."

The next pitch came in, and I heard, "Great, you're one-for-three."

I took off my mask and looked over at Hutchinson.

"Well, I'll tell you one thing," I said. "I'm not going to be oh-for-four, 'cause I'm going to nail you."

I put my mask back on, and after the next pitch he kept up the same patter. I walked over to the Reds' dugout and told him, "Get the hell out. I don't need to listen to your shit."

"Well, I'll go to the league office tomorrow and I'll get your fucking job," he said.

"Well, if you, your brother, or your dad can get my job," I said, "I don't want the fucking thing. Now, get out of my face!"

A few batters later, I thought I heard the same voice. I looked over at the Reds dugout. Fred wasn't there anymore, but I could see everyone on the bench laughing like hell. And I was thinking, *That's a little odd, 'cause Fred's got himself ejected and he's not there anymore, so it can't be him talking.*

Then I thought, *When I tossed him, Hutch had water all over his chest.* I wondered what he was doing all covered in water.

After that, the next few Reds hitters who came up would dig in, look down, and start laughing. It started driving me nuts. I wondered what was going on. When Reds first baseman Gordy Coleman came to the plate, I decided to ask him. I trusted Gordy. He was a good guy—about the only good guy on their ball club.

When the catcher went out to the mound, I asked, "Gordy, what the hell is going on?" He was bent over so it wouldn't look like we were talking to each other.

"Hutch was getting a drink of water at the end of the dugout when you ran him," Gordy said.

So after a couple more batters I got to thinking, *Hold it a minute. How the hell could he be yelling at me when he was drinking water?*

I called time-out and approached one of the Reds coaches, Reggie Otero.

"Reggie, was that you?" I asked.

All the Reds' players burst out laughing. They thought it was real funny because I had ejected Fred for something his coach had been doing. Turns out that Otero could do a great imitation of Hutchinson's voice. His act impressed me, but as I returned to the plate to dust it off, all of a sudden it occurred to me to call time-out again. I walked back to the dugout.

"Come to think of it," I said to Otero, "I caught you. So you get your ass out of here too!"

Hutch, who could get nasty, taught me another important lesson. As an umpire you always turn the side of your body to the man you're going to eject, because if you don't, he'll leap right in the way of your arm as you're signaling his ejection and swear that you hit him. And that can get you in the deep shithouse with the president of the league. I learned that the hard way.

"Get out of here," I yelled at Hutchinson, tossing him out of the game. But I didn't turn sideways when I made the motion to toss him, and I accidentally hit him with my hand.

"You hit me," he said.

"Fuck you," I said.

And that's how I learned you have to turn your side to whomever you're ejecting. Because a guy like Hutchinson will try to put you in the shithouse any way he can.

He reported me to the league office, and I had to go there and explain. I caught hell from everybody. Sure I did.

"Hutch said that you hit him."

What was I going to say? That I didn't hit him? That he walked into my arm? It sounded too much like an excuse.

"I'll have to fine you."

"Do what you have to."

— 11 —

Another thing I learned that first year was that if the manager was an asshole, his players probably would be as well, and that was certainly true of Freddie Hutchinson's Cincinnati Reds.

One of the Reds' worst players to deal with was Frank Robinson, the Hall of Fame outfielder. He was the toughest player I had to face. Frank Robinson was always trouble, but of course Frank Robinson was playing for Freddie Hutchinson.

We were playing a game in Cincinnati in the summer, one of those terribly hot days. Back then the umpires had to wear a coat, so I was out there in the heat with my coat on and I was miserable. The next batter was Frank, and he came up to home plate. He was squeezing the bat and talking to himself.

"Let's go," I said. "It's hot. I don't care for your wasting time. I've got to work out here. Let's go. Get in the box."

Frank didn't move. He just stood there, squeezing his bat.

"You screwed me at first base yesterday," he said, "and you're screwing me now."

"Hey, what the hell's wrong with you?" I said. "What are you talking about, screwing you?"

"You heard me," Frank said. "You screwed me last night, and now you're screwing me again."

"Let's go," I said. "Get in the box."

"I'll get in the box when I want to," said Frank.

"No, you don't understand," I said. "I'm telling you now: Get in the box."

"I'm not getting in the box," said Frank.

"Pitch the ball," I ordered.

The ball hit the catcher's glove. *Wham.*

"Strike one. Now," I said, "will you get in the box?"

"I'm not getting in the box."

"Pitch the ball."

Wham.

"Strike two," I said. "You getting in the box?"

"I'm not getting in the box."

Shag Crawford came down from first base, and he wanted to know what the hell was going on.

"I told the gentleman to get in the box," I said, "and he refused, so I called a strike. And I called strike two."

Shag said to Frank, "Don't be silly. Get in the box."

"I'll get in the box when I want to," he stubbornly said to Shag.

"Well, let me tell you something," said Shag. "I'm going to walk to first base, and if you're not in the box by the time I get there, you're out of here."

"I always thought you were a straight-shooter, Shag," said Robinson, "but you're nothing but a son of a bitch."

So Shag jerked him, threw him out of the ball game.

Dick Sisler, Hutch's right-hand man, came out and called me a son of a bitch, so I ejected him too. Sisler then said to Shag, "If you have the balls, I'll meet you after the game and kick your ass."

This was old-time baseball in the early 1960s. This is what it was like. It was wonderful.

In 1982 Frank Robinson became the manager of the San Francisco Giants, and he was the same pain in the ass he was as a player. Except that as manager he hated to be ejected, because he knew he would have to spend the rest of the game in the dressing room, watching it on TV. He could still get mad—we had a few good arguments—but as manager, I never tossed him.

Speaking of Fred Hutchinson—whom we all despised—Fred had cancer the last two years he managed. And during those two years, he was just as nasty as ever.

One day Ed Vargo ran him.

Hutch was in the third-base dugout and Vargo was at first base, and it took Hutch a good five minutes to walk over there, because he couldn't hardly walk. When he finally got to the dugout he took his time emptying his pockets, and then he had to tell someone he was running the ball club, and then he had to walk all the way from the third-base dugout over to first base.

I was umpiring at second and walked over to first to be a witness, something we were told to do any time one of us got into an argument. I was there to listen. Fred was a bit taller than Ed, and Fred got up really close and looked down at him, and he said, "I hope you get what I've got."

And he turned and walked off.

That was the worst I ever heard. I knew that sometimes they wished we were dead, and this was proof of it.

Fred had to quit as manager in the middle of the '63 season when he became too ill to continue. Not too long after I entered the majors, he died.

One evening in Cincinnati, a writer came into our dressing room before a ball game. He said, "Fellows, I just thought you'd want to know. Fred Hutchinson has died."

"Jesus," said umpire Augie Donatelli, "can you tell me where they buried him?"

"Jeez, Augie," the writer said. "That's really nice." And he started to write the address on a piece of paper.

"Augie, you want to send a card of remembrance?" asked the writer.

"No," said Augie, "I want to go and piss on his grave."

That's what we all thought of Fred Hutchinson.

CHAPTER 10

CHARACTERS

— 1 —

Hutch and the Reds weren't the only thorns in my side that first year. The combination of St. Louis Cardinals manager Red Schoendienst and his ace pitcher Bob Gibson was just as toxic. Red was horrible. He wanted everything in his favor, everything to lean toward him. If a call went against him, you were wrong as an umpire. He'd put you in the shithouse in a minute. That was his attitude. He was not a fair person.

The Cardinals under Red were a bunch of assholes, and Bob Gibson was the biggest asshole. He was the leader. He was also a snake. You know, a snake's nice if you've just fed him a mouse. You're in pretty good shape if you did that. But don't reach in there if he's hungry. He'll eat you. Well, Bob was hungry every time he went to the mound.

All the guys on the club were afraid of him. One time his catcher, Tim McCarver, went out to talk to him, and he screamed at Tim, "What the fuck do you know about pitching? Get behind home plate."

McCarver walked back, his tail between his legs.

We called McCarver "Ironhands," because when Gibson was pitching, he didn't catch a lot of the balls, and the umpire behind him would get beat to shit. Gibson was tough to catch. He'd throw his fastball, and just as it reached the plate it would start to slow down, and then it would jump three inches—monstrous movement. I don't know how he did it. He held the ball by the stitching and threw it hard. The ball would start to slow down and then it would explode, moving one way or the other. And McCarver had a tough time catching him.

When Bob was pitching, he was in another world. Anyone who crossed him was the enemy, and he didn't care for me. He wanted me to give him five inches on either side of the plate, and despite his attempts at intimidation, I flat-out refused to do it. He didn't care a bit for my strike zone, because mine was a true strike zone. Gibson would bitch like hell throughout the whole ball game.

We were in St. Louis, and Gibson (who, along with Sandy Koufax, was perhaps one of the two best pitchers in the league despite his deficiencies in personality) had pitched eight innings of shutout ball with me umpiring behind the plate. He won the game 2–0.

After the game our umpiring crew was in the dressing room. The radio was on, and I could hear Cardinals broadcaster Jack Buck interviewing Gibson after the game.

"Ladies and gentlemen," said Buck, "we have Bob Gibson as our guest. Bob, how are you?"

Gibson said, "I knew yesterday that I would be in trouble today."

"What do you mean, in trouble?" asked Buck.

"When I saw Harvey at first base yesterday," he said, "I knew I'd be in trouble today. He doesn't give me anything."

Now, Gibson had just thrown a two-hitter and won the game. I had fought the rain, did everything I could have done to get the game in, and he had his victory. And he was bitching.

The next day I ran across Mike Shannon, who had played third base for the Cards and was Jack Buck's radio partner.

"Hi, Harv," Mike said.

"Do I get equal time?" I said to him.

"Are you kidding?" he asked.

"No, I'm not kidding."

"Hell, yes," said Shannon, and right there and then we went on the air.

I told the people of St. Louis: "Ladies and gentlemen, I'm an honest man, and Bob Gibson wants five extra inches on both sides of the plate, and I refuse to give it to him. And that's why on occasion I have to eject him. It's the reason we have arguments. Because I'm not going to give him ten inches more than he deserves, and that's what he wants."

Later Shannon told me, "Harv, we got more phone calls and letters after your response than from anyone we ever had on."

"And how did they look at it?" I asked.

"They were all in your favor," Mike said. "There wasn't one who said you were wrong."

"Great," I said. "Then I got my message across."

— 2 —

Red was managing in my first World Series in 1968 against the Detroit Tigers. With the Cardinals leading three games to one, game five pitted the Cards' Nellie Briles against Mickey Lolich of Detroit. St. Louis needed to win only one more game to take the series. The game was played in Tiger Stadium. It was a day game, back when the World Series was still played during the day.

With the Cardinals ahead 3–0 in the fifth inning, the speedy Lou Brock doubled. Julian Javier then hit a single to left field. Brock rounded third as the left fielder, Willie Horton, came up throwing. He threw a pea to Tigers catcher Bill Freehan.

Brock didn't slide. With Freehan in the way, Brock altered his line to the plate, and as he ran past it, Freehan tagged him. I had a perfect view. Brock never touched the plate. He didn't miss by much, perhaps an inch, but I could see the space between the plate and Brock's cleats, and I called him out.

When I called Brock out, it was the turning point in the series, because pictures showed that just before I made my call Tigers manager Mayo Smith was stepping onto the top step of the dugout to take Lolich out of the game. When I called Brock out, he left Lolich in, and Lolich went on to win the game 5–3. The Tigers then won the next two games to win the series four games to three.

I was criticized by National Leaguers for calling Brock out, but when Doug Harvey is umpiring, there is no such thing as a league. I could have called Brock safe just as easily and nobody would have argued. Nobody. But my heart wouldn't let me do it. Had Brock slid, he would have been safe, and I'd have called him safe. But he didn't, and it changed baseball history.

Red came charging out. With Red, whenever the call went against him, you were wrong. Like his star pitcher, there was nothing fair about him in any way.

Red Schoendienst's biggest gripe was that he said I never gave his pitchers the high pitch. Well, you have to understand that whether a pitch is a ball or a strike is determined by where it's located when it goes across the *front* of home plate. And I could never get people to understand that. Batters stand at the rear of the batter's box because they need as much time as they can get to hit the ball. They have perhaps a hundredth of a second to hit it, so they stand as far back as they can. The ball would come downhill from the mound, would be shin-high at the front of the plate, and then as it crossed the plate it would be knee-high. That pitch is a ball, and as a result Red would be complaining, "Harvey never calls anything above the belt line."

Well, that wasn't true, but I couldn't get Red to understand that.

Red moaned and bitched and cried that I wouldn't give his pitchers the high strike, and now they're trying to get the umpires to give the batters the low strike. You can't give them both. An umpire can set himself to give a higher strike by standing up higher. Or you can call a lower strike by bending down more. But by definition you can't do both. They are two different stances. By saying, "We want a bigger strike zone," they are asking for both. Hell, if that's what you want, widen the plate.

I harken back to a conversation I had with Ted Williams when I asked him, "Ted, where would you want the pitchers to throw if you wanted to put on a hitting exhibition?"

"Right up here," he said, indicating the high part of the strike zone. "You don't even have to think about the angle of your bat. It's right in line with hitting a home run."

And because baseball has stopped calling the low strike, pitchers are forced to throw right into the zone where 250-pound batters hit home runs. What baseball needs are umpires who call the good, low strike zone.

Another important thing to note about the strike zone: When I was coming up through the minor leagues, the old saying was, "If you want to make it in the major leagues, you have to have a pitcher's strike zone. You have to open up your strike zone." To me that means you're cheating for the pitcher, and I don't know how to cheat in any direction. I absolutely made the ball touch the plate if it was going to be a strike. And, of course, it also had to be the right height.

I'm a great believer in fairness. I absolutely was a fair umpire, and yet when I see another umpire opening up his strike zone, I understand why he's doing it. He wants the game to go faster, and I don't mind it. But I wouldn't do that. My heart wouldn't let me do it, because it wouldn't be fair to the batter. I always made sure the pitcher had fairness and the batter had fairness.

"If you're a pitcher's umpire, you won't have as many arguments," I was advised. In other words, the batter will only be up there a short time, but the pitcher will be around for as many as nine innings, and if he isn't happy, he could be screaming at you for nine innings.

Screw it, I said to myself. *I'll take their arguments and stand on my own.*

Arguments are part of baseball. The players and managers need to vent. Anyone who doesn't understand why players get upset and argue has never played the game. I played, so I understand how the players feel. I know what drives them.

— 3 —

My first year I also learned there were gentlemen in the league. One player who was completely fair was Los Angeles Dodgers pitcher Don Drysdale. In one of my first plate jobs during my first season, the Dodgers were playing St. Louis in Sportsman's Park, and Don threw a pitch that the Cards' Stan Musial hit over the big screen in front of the stands and clear over the stands. It was a blast.

Drysdale walked down from the mound and said, "Hey, Doug," which impressed me, because he had taken the time to learn my name.

"Yes," I said.

"Ask Musial if that hurt his hands, will you?" said Drysdale.

I had expected him to ask, "Where was the pitch?" But he never did that. Don and Sandy Koufax were two of the greatest professionals ever to play the game.

— 4 —

One of the most important lessons I learned as an umpire occurred during my rookie season. Gene Mauch was the manager of the Philadelphia Phillies, and he fancied himself a genius with the rules. It was a night game, and I was umpiring at third, and there was a close play. Don Hoak, whom the Phils had acquired from Pittsburgh toward the end of his career, got the ball in time ahead of the sliding runner. He put his glove down, and when the runner came within two feet of him he pulled the glove back, missing the tag, and I called the runner safe.

Mauch came running out to raise hell with me, so I had to run him, and I had to run Hoak as well.

At the end of the evening I had a sore throat from all the hollering. Mauch and I must have stood there for twenty minutes hollering at each other. Finally Al Barlick came over, took charge, and got Mauch to leave the field.

Sitting in a bar that night, I asked myself, *I wonder what would happen if I refused to argue with him?*

The next night I was at second base. There was a slide play there. Phillies second baseman Cookie Rojas caught the ball in time, but I called the runner safe, and out came Mauch again.

This time I stood there with my arms crossed and stared at him. I started counting to twenty to myself—*one, two, three, four . . .* until I got to *eighteen, nineteen, twenty*, and when Mauch started repeating himself, I said to him, "Gene, I've listened to you. Why don't you listen to me?"

Mauch shut up.

"Cookie had the ball in time," I said, "but he had a slow glove and missed the tag."

Gene turned toward Rojas—I was wondering what Cookie was going to say—and with his Spanish accent Rojas said, "He's right, skeeper."

I turned and saw Mauch loping across the infield back to the dugout. He jumped over the foul line and went into the dugout, and that was the last argument I ever had with him. He accepted the fact that I knew what I was doing.

I understand that years later, when Mauch was managing Montreal, he got in a big fight on the field and told the umpiring crew, "I'll trade one Doug Harvey for all of you."

Bless his heart, when I saw Cookie at a Baseball Assistance Team dinner a few years ago, I told him I'd never forget his backing me up as long as I live.

"You could've hung me out to dry," I said. "And if you had, I'd have run your ass too."

We both had a good laugh about it.

But after that, I adopted what I call the Harvey Twenty-Second Rule. It relates to demeanor, something I teach to young umpires, though not everyone can carry it off.

When I see a young umpire out there screaming and hollering at a manager or a player, I say to him, "What are you screaming about, son? What are you so uptight about? I'm watching you and you're screaming and hollering."

"Well, he's screaming and hollering at me," the answer always comes back.

"And how many men does it take to make an argument?" I ask.

"Well, it takes two."

And then I say, "One option is for you to refuse to argue. Just stand there and count to twenty. He will have exhausted himself screaming and hollering. Let him do it. But don't let him get up in your face. Tell him, 'Hold it. Hold it.' He will look at you funny.

"Tell him, 'I'm listening to you, but back up or I'm going to jerk your ass out of here.' And you'll be surprised. Never once did a manager or player tell me, 'I'm not backing up.' You tell him, 'I can hear. My hearing is very good, but I refuse to listen to you if you're going to scream and holler in my face. Now what is it you want to tell me?'

"And that's when you give him twenty seconds to talk. After that you say, 'Now it's my turn. I've listened to you, haven't I?'

"'Yeah, you listened to me.'

"'Well, I think it's only right that you listen to me.'

"'Okay.'

"And then you explain yourself.

"'I was in perfect position. I was right there. I saw the ball come in. I saw the tag. There's no doubt in my mind he missed the tag, and I have to call him safe, and safe he's going to stay.'

"'Goddamn it,' he might start in again.

"'No no no,' I would say. 'You don't understand. I listened to you, and you listened to me, and now this conversation is over.'

"'What do you mean?'

"'I mean if you don't get away from me, I'm going to jerk your ass out of this ball game.'"

Now it's in his lap. He has a choice. He can stay out there and get tossed. Or he can return to the dugout.

Finally, I instruct young umpires, "If you can get rid of the screaming and hollering, you got them by the balls."

Many can't do it. I told this to Jerry Crawford when he first came up, and he said to me, "Chief, I know what you're trying to tell me. I understand. But I just can't umpire that way."

Years later he came back to me and said, "It took me a long time, but I finally understand that yours is the easier way to umpire."

— 5 —

Two years after our screaming match, Gene Mauch was the manager of the Phillies when they made their infamous dive, losing most of their games at the end of the 1964 season to lose the pennant to the St. Louis Cardinals. That year Jocko Conlan was my crew chief, and Jocko was going to retire at the end of the year. Ordinarily, the league assigned our umpiring crew to many of the Phillies games, but because everyone thought the race was over and was sure the Phillies were going to win it, the league sent us to the West Coast to umpire a series between Houston and the Dodgers. Meanwhile, the Phillies kept losing, and by the end of the season Mauch and the Phillies had blown it.

It was such a surprise. Mauch screwed around with the pitching staff, pitching Jim Bunning and Chris Short almost every game it seemed. He panicked and pitched guys out of turn, and Gene just caught hell from everybody. But it was Gene Mauch who taught me that important lesson: It takes two to make a fight.

— 6 —

I had an incident involving Herman Franks, the manager of the Chicago Cubs, that taught me another lesson I never forgot. I was behind the plate and he said something about the strike zone, and I told him, "Just sit still and leave me alone. I know what I'm doing." And I punched the batter out. Strike three. And he hollered, "Well, you've fucked up everything. Now you're screwing up the strike zone."

Boom, bam, boom. "Get the hell out," and I tossed him. Herman just sat there and looked at me. I said, "Let's go. Let's go." He reached into his back pocket very calmly, took his lineup out, and handed it to Peanuts Lowrey. They were sitting and talking, and I finally got peeved, walked down the third-base line, and got near the bag.

"Let's go, Herman," I said.

He walked to the top step of the dugout, continued across to the third-base area, and we were talking.

"Doug, I didn't curse you."

"Don't give me that, Herman. I was looking right at you when you did it."

He said, "What did you think I called you?"

Translating his words, I said, "You called me a fucking asshole."

"Oh no," he said, "I was saying that was an asshole call." He was improvising.

"I'll tell you what," I said. "I know you think I'm a dingbat, but get the hell out of here—now."

"But, Doug—" he said, and he turned and started walking toward home plate, talking to me. Only I didn't follow him. I was standing at third base and I let him walk. And there Herman was, walking all the way to home plate, thinking he was talking to me. I had crossed my arms and was standing at third base, and now the people were starting to giggle. It was funny. Herman was walking to home plate talking to me, and I wasn't there.

Finally, Franks turned around to have his last say, when to his chagrin he realized that I wasn't there. When he looked back at third, I turned my head and looked out to center field with my arms crossed, like I didn't know he was gone. Oh, jeez. He got so goddamn mad. He came running back, charging me like a wounded buffalo. That day I learned that when you eject a man, you never stand on any dirt. You always stand on grass. They can't kick dirt on you if you're not on dirt. Herman Franks was the only man during my career who ever kicked dirt on me. When he did that, of course, I got him the hell out of the ball game.

The next day, the phone rang in the umpires' dressing room, and Jerry Crawford answered it.

"Chief," he said, "it's Herman."

"You're shitting me."

"No."

"Give me the goddamn phone."

"Yeah?" I said.

"Oh, Doug—you of all people," said Herman. "How could I ever have done that?"

"I don't know," I said.

"Could you see it in your heart to forgive me?" he asked with real contrition.

"Fuck no," I said, feigning anger, "and I'll tell you something else. If you fuck around with me, I'll nail you every time I see you."

Bam. I hung up.

I told the guys in my crew, "Don't forget what I've always said. You never hold a grudge."

That was the way I umpired. I never held a grudge. But I got Herman thinking: *Will he eject me every time he sees me?*

That's the way I worked.

— 7 —

Ted Simmons, the St. Louis Cardinals' catcher, is the only player I should have tossed but didn't. There was a riot going on, and I was working the plate. Ted was behind the plate, and when the melee broke out, he jumped up and tossed his mask toward the dugout, signaling his intention to get involved.

I turned around to him.

"Let me tell you something, Ted," I said. "If you get in that dugout, you'll stay in the game. If I see you out on that field, I'm going to eject you."

As I started heading toward the pile of bodies near the mound, Simmons said to me, "What the fuck do you know, asshole?"

I was already on the dead run to see if I could break up forty players, so I missed him. I didn't eject him.

After that, I kept my eye out for him, but I never did get him.

Which also showed I never carried a grudge. I may never have forgotten when someone said something to me, but that didn't necessarily mean I acted on it. A grudge eats at you. I never allowed that.

— 8 —

When I came up, I was a little bit of a wiseacre. One of the many lessons I learned early was that I had to watch myself.

I was behind the plate in Chicago. The Cubs were playing the Phillies. The Cubs' pitcher was a big guy, a right-hander named Larry Jackson. Wes Covington was the batter; a great big guy, a strong son of a bitch. He came up with the bases stacked. Jackson got two strikes on Covington, and I told myself, *He'll either try to backdoor with a hard slider, or he'll try to cut it inside.*

Without umpires, the game wouldn't survive. *(Doug Harvey Collection)*

Yankee manager Bob Lemon and me before a game. You always give the manager the choice of whether he's to be tossed or not. *(National Baseball Hall of Fame)*

Terry Cooney, Nick Colosi, Larry Barnett, me, and Dick Stello with managers Tommy Lasorda and Bob Lemon before a game in the 1981 World Series. Tommy could be nasty, but I always kind of liked him. *(National Baseball Hall of Fame)*

The umpiring crew for the 1982 World Series. The players are on their best behavior. You don't get many complaints during the World Series. *(National Baseball Hall of Fame)*

Al Forman (NL), me (NL), Hank Soar (AL), and Bill Valentine (AL) before a game at Cooperstown, New York, in 1965. Gene Mauch managed the Phils, Johnny Keane the Yankees. Gene Mauch taught me an important lesson: It takes two to make a fight. *(National Baseball Hall of Fame)*

Being an umpire is like being a policeman in civilized society. *(National Baseball Hall of Fame)*

I don't believe I have ever made a wrong call. *(Doug Harvey Collection)*

After Roberto Clemente's three thousandth hit I shook his hand and handed him the ball. *(Doug Harvey Collection)*

Gerry Davis, me, Dick Stello, and Eric Gregg. Dick was killed in a freak accident. Eric had a terrible problem with food. *(Doug Harvey Collection)*

It's been fifty-two years now. I couldn't do without her. *(Doug Harvey Collection)*

Me, Joy, and our two sons, Scott and Todd. *(Doug Harvey Collection)*

When I met Joy, she was working at the ballpark selling scorecards and seat cushions. *(Doug Harvey Collection)*

I will cherish my induction into the Hall of Fame until the day I die.

(Doug Harvey Collection)

There were years I went through almost an entire season without tossing a single player or manager. *(Doug Harvey Collection)*

We don't ask for respect; we demand it. *(Doug Harvey Collection)*

But he reversed it. He threw the pitch on the inside corner, but missed it. Covington jerked his leg out of there and I said, "Ball."

The Cubs' catcher was Dick Bertell. So here came the next pitch and sure enough, he threw a goddamned slider, and *bam*, the pitch hit the catcher's glove. But it missed.

"Ball," I said.

And I heard, "Oh, Jesus Christ, Harvey."

"Whoa, big fella," I said to Bertell. "We're going the wrong way. Don't be doing that."

Jackson threw another close fastball. I said, "Ball." And Bertell dropped down on his knees and said, "Oh, why?"

I leaned forward and said, "I wanted to see how high the pitcher could jump after I made that call."

"You cocksucker!" said Bertell.

Here we go. The catcher, the pitcher, the manager, the third-base coach: I threw them all out of there. That night, I went out and got drunk.

The next day, at seven o'clock in the morning, the phone rang. It was the head of umpires, Fred Fleig, the man who gave me my job.

"Doug," he said, "I want you to meet me at the hotel."

"Okay," I said groggily, "but you better have some sweet rolls and some coffee, because I'll need them."

I grabbed a cab and headed over to his hotel. We were having coffee and sweet rolls, and he said, "Bertell said you told him you wanted to see how high the pitcher could jump."

"That's right, Mr. Fleig," I said. "That's what I told him."

"Well, I respect you for telling me the truth," he said. "You're kind of a wise kid, and I'm telling you: Get rid of it."

"I'll try," I said. And I did try.

After that, every time Fred would come into a dressing room, he would tell the young umpires, "You listen to what Harv says. He's an honest man, and he won't get you in trouble."

The fact that I always told the truth worked out for me.

— 9 —

My first year in the major leagues was memorable for so many reasons. I entered baseball the same year as Casey Stengel and the Amazin' Mets. They were called the Amazin' Mets as something of a joke. The 1962 Mets may well have been the worst team to come along in quite a while. When the league expanded, the powers that be allowed the existing teams to protect almost all of their decent players, making only over-the-hill veterans and fringe ballplayers available to the two new teams, the Mets and the Houston Colt .45's.

During a game at the Polo Grounds, there was a play at second base. I called the runner safe when the Mets second baseman was late with a tag. Casey came trotting out to protest. In that deep voice of his, he said, "Young man, it appeared to me that the second baseman had the ball and tagged the man coming in, and therefore I feel he should be out."

"Casey, let me tell you something," I said. "Your fielder caught the ball, but he was reaching forward instead of catching it coming backward, so it took time for him to reach forward and catch the ball, and then he put a slow tag on him."

"A slow tag?" said Casey.

"Yeah, Casey, that's right. A slow tag."

Casey turned around and started to walk off, and I could hear him muttering under his breath. Both his hands were up in the air, and he was saying, "Slow tag. Slow bats. Slow arms."

Casey was a wonderful gentleman. I loved him.

— 10 —

As great as Casey was, that's how opposite-of-great his successor, Wes Westrum, was. Wes was a pain in the ass. He would get pissed off at me all the time. He was always trying to prove me wrong. One time he told me, "Harvey, I'm going to be watching the replay on the TV."

One game he came out to argue with me four times.

He kept saying to me, "I'm going to check the TV."

"Westrum," I told him, "I'm better than any fuckin' TV you got."

Finally, I ran him. I couldn't take it any longer.

— 11 —

We used to have to work old-timers' day games. Whoever wasn't working the plate that day would umpire for three innings for the old-timers. We were in New York at the new Shea Stadium. Roger Craig was on the mound and Joe DiMaggio was the batter, and Roger came over and said to me, "Harvey, if you strike Joe DiMaggio out, I'll kill you. Pull it in."

"For Christ's sake, you think I have no sense at all," I said. "As far as I'm concerned, the gentleman gets eight strikes."

They announced Joe's name, and we waited and waited, and we could see him standing around in the dugout. Finally he came out and said, "I'm sorry. I couldn't find a bat."

"No problem, Joe."

Later Felipe Alou told me, "Joe couldn't find a bat, so he took mine. It was the heaviest bat in the rack."

On the first pitch he hit a one-hopper off the center-field wall. It was a wonderful thing to see. He swung so smoothly, didn't put any effort into it. But his legs were gone, and first base was as far as he could go. I thought to myself, *For a guy to drive the ball that far with bad legs like that—what a shame he isn't young. I would have loved to have seen him in his youth.*

Joe DiMaggio used to play in our golf tournaments, and there's never been a nicer gentleman in all the world. But he had to be comfortable around the people he was with.

In spring training, Joe was a coach with the Oakland A's. I

was umpiring at third base, and Joe was sitting on the edge of the home dugout by third base, and he let out a fart, a big one.

The lady sitting right above him said, "What was that?"

Her husband said, "What was what?"

She said, "Didn't you hear it? There's something wrong with this place."

I looked over and Joe's face was as red as a Cincinnati Reds uniform. He was blushing to high heaven.

— 12 —

When I came up in 1962, Alvin Dark was the manager of the San Francisco Giants. I was umpiring a game at third base in Milwaukee a couple years later, and Jim Ray Hart of the Giants hit a ball way out to left field. The bases were loaded and there were two outs in a close ball game.

The ball Hart hit was one of those balls I felt was going to be close as to whether it left the ballpark or not. I busted my ass, got halfway out there, and set myself—which you always have to do. Any umpire who tries to umpire on the run is a damn fool. You *have* to set yourself.

I set myself and watched the ball come down. And this is another Harvey theory: Don't watch the ball when it's on its way down—instead, when it's still twenty feet high, watch the fielder's glove; you'll never miss whether it's caught or not. The rule also goes for the fielder charging in and taking the ball off his shoe top. If you leave the ball when it's twenty feet in the air and watch the fielder's glove, you'll never miss whether it's a trap or not.

"You'll always be able to make that call," I tell all my young people.

This ball was coming down. Rico Carty, the left fielder, ran back to the fence and jumped up. If I had been following the ball, I wouldn't have been able to keep up with it. The ball always leads your eyes, so you don't see what happens.

I left the ball and went to the glove, and goddamn if I didn't see a fan in the stands holding a small, brown-colored stick of some sort—it could have been a piece of steel or it could have been a pencil—sticking out over the edge of the stands. The ball hit it just as Rico Carty leaped up trying to catch the ball.

I ran out and saw the fan pull back this stick. And I called Jim Ray Hart out, citing fan interference.

Al Dark came running out near third base, and he wanted to argue. Whitey Lockman was his third-base coach. Whitey came over and said, "Skip, I hate to tell you, but Harv's right."

That was the first time I ever had a ballplayer say something to save me. It happened two or three times later during my career.

I never did have any bad arguments with Al.

Another manager I rarely got into a bad argument with was Pittsburgh Pirates manager Danny Murtaugh. Danny was crusty but fair. He would come out and argue, but he was one of those managers who never wanted to come out of the ball game. He wanted to be on the field, so he kept his cool to keep from getting ejected.

Harry Craft of the Colt .45's didn't like to argue. He didn't have the fire in his belly. He wanted things to go smoothly and didn't argue at all.

Bobby Bragan, the Milwaukee manager, never argued with me, and there was a reason for it. Bobby managed in the Pacific Coast League when I was umpiring there. I had known him, so when he came in we respected each other. I also knew Bobby Cox from the minors. He had been a player in the California League in the early 1960s. He was at Reno playing second base. That's how far back we went. I read that Bobby got tossed more than any other manager in the history of the National League. I couldn't believe it. I never ran Bobby once.

One manager who could be nasty was the Cardinals' Johnny Keane. There was a to-do at third base involving Tony Venzon, and I walked over from second base to listen in. Keane had started the argument and then stood directly behind Venzon, listening to his every word, hoping to catch him saying something wrong.

"Hey, Tony," I said, "it's me, Harv. You won't believe who's standing right behind you."

He turned around quickly, and when he saw Keane standing there he unloaded a string of expletives.

"If you want to argue with me," said Tony, "you better get the hell over here in front where I can see you. Don't you ever—"

And on and on he went. Tony turned the argument around on Keane.

Most of the arguments I had came in my first few years. One of the reasons they eventually stopped was that the players saw that I demanded respect. They learned quickly that if you called me anything but *sir, Mr. Umpire,* or *Doug,* you'd be ejected.

The first player I ever ejected was Joe Torre, who was just breaking in as a catcher for the St. Louis Cardinals. They were playing the Pirates in St. Louis toward the end of the season. With two out, Joe hit a double, a runner was coming in to score, and it was going to be close. I was umpiring at second base. Joe rounded second, and I saw him touch the bag. He ran past it by about ten feet, then turned to look to home plate to see if there was going to be a tag play just as Pirate catcher Smoky Burgess—who had come halfway out to the mound—caught the ball and fired it back to second, catching Torre by surprise.

"You're out," I called.

"You're full of shit," Torre said.

"What?" I said.

"You son of a bitch," he said.

"You're out of here," I said, making Joe Torre the first player I ever ejected.

After I ran Torre, the Cardinals' third base coach came running out to second base.

"Why did you toss Torre?" he demanded.

"He called me a son of a bitch."

"Why, young man," said the coach, "this is the major leagues. You have to be able to take it when you're up here."

Just about then Al Barlick walked over and got between us.

"You're out of line," he said to the coach. "Get back to your bench."

Like a schoolboy, he turned and walked back to the dugout.

— 13 —

They also found out that if you screwed with me—which I considered another form of disrespect—I not only wouldn't take it, I would get even. Once word got around that I was no guy to mess with, most of the trash-talking stopped.

As an example, our crew was in Cincinnati for a game against San Francisco. Johnny Edwards was catching for the Reds and Tom Haller was catching for the Giants, and I was arguing balls and strikes pretty good with both of them.

Haller was batting and he yelled down to Edwards, "Hey, maybe you and I ought to call balls and strikes. Ha-ha-ha-ha-ha."

I was burning. I didn't do or say a thing. I just waited my turn.

Late in a close ball game, Haller came to bat. There were two men on base, and the Giants were down one run. The pitcher looked in and wound up, and just as he was starting his delivery,

I said just loud enough for Haller and Edwards to hear, "So, you think you can umpire? You wouldn't make a pimple on a fucking umpire's ass. Strike one."

Haller didn't even swing. He backed out when I started talking. He looked at me with a funny look on his face, and he stepped back into the box. He figured I had had my say. Well, when the pitcher started to wind up, I knew he couldn't step out, and I let him have it again.

"I could take you people and give you six years of training, and you couldn't make a fucking umpire," I said as he swung at this one. The ball was outside. He shouldn't have swung at it. Now he was thinking that I intended to screw him on every pitch, which I did.

Haller stepped back and said, "Hey, Harv, I realize we had some fun with you. But this is really an important part of the game."

I just stared at him.

"Let's go."

And he stepped into the box.

"Yeah," I said, "this is a really important part of the game, and nobody can hear me but you two assholes. Shall we play baseball? What do you want to do?"

And just as the pitcher started to deliver, I said, "Oh, by the way, the last ball you swung at was a ball."

And Haller swung at a pitch over his head for strike three. He threw the bat down and walked away.

Now it was Johnny Edwards's turn to come to bat with a runner on first. He looked at me. The first pitch came in. I didn't say a word. I called it a strike. On the next pitch he swung at a ball over his head and popped it up. So I got my revenge. And I did it in a way that let the two players involved know not to fuck with me again, without me making a big scene about it. This is what baseball needs. It needs people who are mature enough to handle the situation without screaming.

Another time I read in the paper a statement from Bill White, the first baseman who had just been traded to the Philadelphia Phillies, that the umpiring was all fucked up. He said that the only good umpires in the league were Al Barlick, Jocko Conlan, and Shag Crawford.

"The rest," he said, "are terrible."

The next time I was behind the plate when the Phils were playing, Bill came to bat, and on the first pitch, which was outside, I called, "Strike one."

"Wasn't that pitch outside?" Bill asked.

"It might have been," I said, "but as terrible an umpire as I am, who the hell would know?"

I didn't say another word, but you better believe he started swinging at anything that was close. It's amazing what you can do if you use your head instead of your voice. Use your damn brain. That's what I teach young umpires.

CHAPTER 11

SANDY, WILLIE, AND CHARLIE HUSTLE

— 1 —

My career let me work alongside some of the greatest ballplayers ever. As for pitchers, if I had to fight the devil in a game for every soul, I'd take Sandy Koufax. If I knew Sandy was going to be pitching, I couldn't wait to get to the ballpark. You knew he was going to be around the plate. Scientists will tell you that it is impossible for a pitched ball to rise. Well, if Koufax's fastball didn't rise, then I have to say it came in at one angle and changed angles upward. Because just as the batter started to swing, that ball went up. Sandy threw his fastball dead overhand from a high mound, and it just exploded up.

Sandy was also a gentleman. One day he had two strikes on a batter and threw a curveball. I called it a ball. He took the ball back from the catcher, and he looked in at me, and he took his left hand and put it flat against his chest as if to ask, *Was it too high?*

I nodded yes. He threw the next pitch six inches lower. Bingo. I nailed him. Strike three. That's how good he was.

Shag Crawford was umpiring behind the plate in the 1963 World Series, and he told me that Sandy had two strikes on Mickey Mantle and threw a fastball around his chin. He said the next one came the same way, chin high, and catcher John Roseboro caught it just below the knees. The pitch had a dynamite break on it, and it just left Mantle standing at home plate, strike three. And Mantle couldn't believe it.

I flew into New York after a game in Chicago and was watching the Yankees play the Washington Senators on TV. They were interviewing Mantle, and the color guy was saying to him that in his opinion Carlos Pascual had to have the absolute best curveball in baseball.

Mickey smiled and said, "Have you ever heard of a pitcher by the name of Koufax?"

Until the day Koufax retired, no one knew how much pain he had to endure when he pitched. I had a bad back that I had injured in junior college. It would constantly go out of place, and Bill Buhler, the trainer for the Dodgers, was the only one—I tried several—who knew what he was doing and could put it back in place for me. Because of that, I would go see him when the ball club was out on the field taking infield and batting practice before the game.

I walked in one day and Bill, who was wearing rubber gloves, was rubbing down Koufax, and I could smell something really foul.

"What the hell is that?" I asked.

"It's Capsolin," Bill said.

Capsolin is an ugly bloodred before the air gets to it, and he was rubbing this stuff across Sandy's chest and on his shoulder clear down to his left arm, almost to the elbow. I couldn't believe Sandy was putting himself through that type of torture just so he could pitch. When Sandy finally quit at age thirty after winning twenty-seven games in the 1966 season, it really didn't surprise me. Sandy was suffering tremendously. I know, because when I was in high school I was elected to the letterman's club, and as part of their hazing they would rub this Capsolin on your balls. It hurt so much I didn't sleep all night. I had to put ice on my balls, and that's how I spent the whole night, and the pain didn't ease until the next day. I would never want anyone to have to go through that.

Sandy Koufax was the best pitcher I ever saw. I'd pitch him against any pitcher in the world, against any pitcher in history. That's how good he was. I just thank God he gave me the opportunity to umpire on the days Sandy Koufax pitched. In all of baseball, I'm not sure we'll ever see the likes of him again.

— 2 —

Another great pitcher who was a gentleman was St. Louis Cardinals and Philadelphia Phillies pitcher Steve Carlton. Steve was very, very quiet.

Great ballplayers don't say anything. They don't worry to themselves, *Gee, it's a 3-and-2 pitch. I thought I had it.* They don't scream at the umpire. They figure, *If it's 3-and-2 and the umpire called ball four, it must have been outside. There's another batter up there. Let's go get him.*

Man, Carlton could pitch. A left-hander, he'd take that hard slider and break it in on a right-handed batter. It broke hard and caught the plate. The batters would start swinging and from behind the plate I could see they were missing because the ball had such great movement. They were swinging over the damned thing. Hell, they were fortunate to get a foul ball off of him, never mind a base hit. Carlton was one of the greatest pitchers of our time.

— 3 —

We knew that Nolan Ryan had a special arm. When he first came up with the New York Mets I wondered whether he'd ever be able to capture the strike zone. He had problems. He couldn't throw strikes. And then the Mets traded him over to the American League for Jim Fregosi of the Angels. The Mets never could find a decent third baseman, and they were hoping Fregosi could do the job. Unfortunately, Jim didn't play much, and Nolan went into the Hall of Fame.

The reason he became a sudden star with the California Angels was that the American League gave the high strike because the umpires wore the outside chest protector, and it didn't matter that everything he threw was up. He blew through the league. Once he was given the high strike, the batters had to swing at anything within six inches of it. And when he finally learned to control his pitches, he came back to the National League and did just fine.

— 4 —

Another pitcher who was outstanding when he came up to the majors was Fernando Valenzuela of the Los Angeles Dodgers. I never had any arguments with Fernando, because he didn't speak English and I don't speak Spanish. When he pitched he never looked at the catcher. He was interesting. He could spin that ball in the opposite direction as good as any screwball pitcher I ever saw.

He became a star and a hero, and then suddenly after he became a hero in Mexico, he quit working at it during the off-season, because when he came back, suddenly his screwball didn't break as much as it did before, and the batters started to hit him.

Before that, Fernando was really great.

— 5 —

Dwight Gooden was 24-4 with a 1.53 ERA in 1985. He had a dynamite fastball and slider. He could hum it. He knew how to pitch up and down, in close, away. He was outstanding.

With a guy like that, there were very few arguments. When a guy wins that many games, what the hell is there to argue about? An occasional pitch, maybe. Is he going to get mad and blow the game? Come on. You're not going to do that. That's when the manager tells the pitcher, "If the umpire needs his ass chewed, I'll come out and do it. Don't you say a word."

Dwight knew how to pitch and he knew how to act. He was a pleasure. I enjoyed working with him that year. He was so *on*. He was like Sandy Koufax.

— 6 —

Greg Maddux was another guy who got the absolute most out of what he had. Here's a guy who wasn't overpowering, but he could put the ball exactly where it belonged. I got such a kick because everyone said, "The umpires give him extra on the plate." Not so. Not so at all. The man was good enough that he could put that sucker there and move it just enough that the batter would think, "That's off the plate," and it would be strike one.

The next one he'd say, "There's the same pitch," and he'd swing at it, and the damn thing would break inside and they'd foul it off for strike two.

He'd throw one up and tight to back the batter off the plate, then throw a little slider on the other side of the plate, strike three.

It was really something to sit back and watch. He was another of the pitchers like Koufax and so many others who didn't complain. He worked his job. He wasn't overpowering and yet he got people out. He kept his mouth shut. The umpires just adored looking out to the bullpen and seeing him warming up. It was wonderful when you had a pitcher like Koufax or Maddux, who never said anything and just threw strikes. It makes it so much easier on the umpire.

You get through and you feel, *I've had some kind of a day*. But *you* haven't had a day. You just reported the fact that the *pitcher* had a hell of a day.

— 7 —

The umpire is there for one reason and one reason only: To make sure one team doesn't gain an unfair advantage. It's that simple. For the game to have meaning it has to be fair, and the only thing standing between fairness and chaos is the umpiring crew.

You'll be shocked and maybe disappointed when I expose the horseshit players who tried and got caught cheating, using everything from phantom tags and corked bats to scuffed baseballs. I'll even shine a light on umpires who compromised their integrity. You think managers wouldn't cheat if they could win a few more games? You think pitchers don't cheat? Man, you have to watch those bastards every minute.

I used to get a kick out of Tommy Lasorda. He'd come waddling out. He could be nasty but I always kind of liked him. In this game, Don Sutton, who was a hell of a pitcher when he wasn't cheating, was pitching for the Dodgers, and he was pitching a brand-new ball. He rubbed it up, and there was a fly out and Jerry Crawford got the ball and looked at it, and he called me over.

"Chief, look at this," Jerry said. And he showed the ball to me, and it had a scab right on the league president's signature. I didn't think it was an accident that the mark had been put on that spot.

When a ball is marked in a specific place, the pitcher knows right where to grip it to make it more than slide. He can make it drop. What a major league pitcher can do with a marked ball is magic. And it's cheating.

Sutton pitched another brand-new ball, and on his first pitch Ken Reitz hit a fly out to Rick Monday in center field. Monday flipped the ball to Jerry coming in, and Jerry called me over again. That ball had been scuffed in the same spot as the other one.

"Lasorda, come out here," I said.

Tommy came out.

"Look at this ball."

"Yeah? So?"

"Do you see this scuff right here?" I asked.

"Yeah."

"Well, someone on your ball club is marring the ball"—I didn't even say that Sutton was the one marring it—"and I have to think Sutton is pitching the marred ball knowing it's marred, and I'm telling you, if he does it again, I'm going to toss him."

"Jesus Christ, Harvey," Lasorda said. "What are you trying to be, God? You can't do that."

"Yes I can," I said, "and I will."

Sure enough, in the bottom of the sixth Sutton pitched another brand-new ball, and the batter hit another fly out to Monday in center.

"Rick, give me that ball," I ordered him.

I'll never forget the look on Monday's face. He had a silly, shit-eating grin. There was a scar on the ball in the same spot as the others, and as Sutton was walking off the field, I told him,

"Keep going." Right then and there I threw him out of the ball game.

Out came Lasorda, ready to do battle.

Sutton, meanwhile, went into the dressing room, and when he came out he was holding a legal form letter.

"My lawyer will be in touch with you," he said.

He laid the letter on my arm. I should have folded it up and kept it for posterity. Instead I tore it into a million pieces. If he wasn't cheating, why was he carrying around the piece of paper?

"Fuck you, and your lawyer too," I told Sutton.

"Harvey," said Lasorda, "what are you trying to do?"

"Tommy," I said, "I'm trying to clean up this game a little bit."

"The last guy I ever saw who tried to clean up a town," said Lasorda, "was Wyatt fucking Earp."

It was a great line, and it took all of my power to keep from breaking out laughing. But this was serious, and I had to carry out what I was doing.

I had told the other umpires on my crew, "Don't get mad. Get even. Wait your turn. There will come a time."

Six years later, I got my chance with Lasorda.

I was in Pittsburgh and the Pirates were playing Lasorda's Dodgers. Rick Rhoden, who once was a Dodger pitcher and a teammate of Don Sutton, was pitching for the Pirates, and he was sticking it to the Dodgers.

In the middle of the game between innings, Lasorda whistled at me to get my attention.

"Harv," he said.

I turned and looked at him.

"Come on over here."

"I don't go to dugouts," I said. "If you want to see me, you come out here."

Lasorda came out, and he was carrying five balls with him.

"Look at these balls," he said.

I picked one up and looked at it. I looked at a couple more and pretended I didn't see the scuffs that Rhoden had apparently put on them.

"Those are National League balls," I said. "That's what we're using."

"No, no," said Tommy. "That's not what I'm saying. Here, look at this. Look!"

He was showing me where the balls were scuffed.

"Now, Tommy," I said with utmost sincerity, "where do you think Rhoden learned that?"

"I don't give a damn where he learned that," Tommy said. "I want you to clean it up."

"Well, Tommy," I said, "the last guy I ever saw clean up a town was Wyatt fucking Earp."

Tommy dropped the five balls on home plate and walked back to the dugout without saying another word, and he didn't come out again during the rest of the ball game.

It's exactly what I always tried to tell the young umpires. I'd say, "Don't get all pissed off. Just listen and eject them if they have to be ejected, and if they really put your ass to the wall, just wait. There will come a day when justice will be yours."

That's why I respected Hall of Fame pitchers like Don Drysdale and Steve Carlton so much. They did it without cheating. They didn't have to cheat.

— 8 —

I never told anyone, but I almost quit after the first Sutton incident. Clearly Sutton was cheating. Why would he be carrying a letter like that if he *wasn't* cheating? I reported to the league office that there was one smudge on each of three league balls, and the balls never hit the ground. They had been hit and caught by a fielder. Sutton was caught red-handed.

There was a hearing. Sutton took his lawyer, his manager, and his general manager, and they all went and hammered Chub Feeney, the president of the National League, and Feeney decided they must have been scuffed by the ground or maybe before they left the ball bag. They gave all kinds of excuses. Feeney let Sutton off with a slap on the wrist.

My next game was in Montreal, and as I stood there at third base I was so upset that Sutton wasn't suspended or fined that I couldn't keep the tears from coming to my eyes. I was talking to myself, telling myself that I ought to quit and go home. That's how upset I was.

In the tenth inning, the Expos had a runner on third and two outs. I was still crying when the Philadelphia pitcher balked. It should have won the game for Montreal. Gary Carter, who was on third base, screamed at me, "Harvey, he balked."

But I had tears in my eyes, and I was so choked up I never saw it. When he balked, I was at the point where I was going to break out crying, because the decision had been so disrespectful to the game of baseball.

After the game, I told Joy that I was going to quit, but she talked me out of it.

"Stay with it a couple of days and see if you still feel that way," she said.

I held a meeting with my umpiring crew and told them what Feeney had decided. They were almost as despondent as I was.

"Let me tell you something," I said. "I don't want you looking at any ball. If anyone shows you, throw it out, because we tried—we did our job—and they didn't back us up, so screw it. We're not going to throw any balls out."

And that's what we did the rest of the year.

I went back to umpiring, but, man, that hurt me. To think I had done it properly, and because Sutton had a lawyer and a manager and his general manager, he got off. Nah, that was no good. I mean, it hurt me clear to my heart. I knew the guy was cheating and they refused to back me.

— 9 —

Then there was Gaylord Perry, a Hall of Famer and the cleverest motherfucker I ever saw. He threw a spitter, which is illegal. He could load that thing up. We knew he was putting some kind of shit on the ball. We just couldn't catch him. We were in San Francisco and Gaylord was pitching. Shag Crawford said to me, "All right, keep your eye on me. When I see him turn his back to me to rub up a new ball, you come running, and we're going to catch that son of a bitch."

I ran in and he still had his head down, rubbing up the ball, and I took the ball. I rubbed my hands on his shirt and we found—absolutely nothing. I don't know what he did.

A few years ago, I saw him at the Hall of Fame ceremonies. I had to find out.

"Gaylord," I said. "Tell me, how did you do it? Where did you hide that shit?"

"What shit, Harv?"

"C'mon. I have to know before I die."

"Magic, Harv, magic."

"Gaylord."

"Well, maybe we'll sit down one day and have a talk."

I'm still waiting.

Chub Feeney, who had been the Giants' general manager and was Giant owner Horace Stoneham's nephew, became the president of the National League in 1970. When he took over, he announced, "We're going to chase all the spitballers out of our league."

He told the umpires, "If a ball acts like a spitball, if it's a strike, I want you to call it a ball. If the batter hits it for an out, you bring the batter back."

And that's what we did in spring training, and all of them who were using the spitter jumped over to the American League. And then within two years the American League did the same thing. They were chased right out of baseball.

Gaylord Perry came out with his own solution to the problem. He was pitching for the San Diego Padres, and the son of a bitch invented the puffball. He had the grounds crew put a huge resin bag on the mound in San Diego. It was dry resin, and he would take it and bounce it in his hand, and then he'd take the ball and put it in his hand, and when he pitched it, the ball would come out of a puff of white smoke so the batter couldn't pick it up right away. It was distracting to the batter, but what was funny about it was that the batters never said a word about it. They figured he was just using resin.

I always said, "Gaylord Perry is the cleverest son of a bitch I ever saw."

— 10 —

I saw some wonderful hitters as well. As far as I'm concerned, Willie Mays was the best player I ever saw. I came up when he was still in his prime. What an amazing athlete. It's just a shame that he had to play so many games in Candlestick Park. Anywhere else, he would've broken Babe Ruth's home-run record.

I can recall a game in which Willie slid into third base trying to beat the throw, and Jocko Conlan called him out. After Willie slid in, he leaped up and put both his hands on Jocko's chest. Very slowly, Jocko looked down at his chest, and let me tell you, I never saw a player run so fast in all his life. Willie took off for the bench—which was on the first-base line—and didn't stop until he reached the dugout. He did that because he knew if he had waited around any longer, Jocko would have run him. Jocko didn't give a shit who he ran.

People think umpires have favorites. I'll tell you who our favorites are: The ones who can keep their mouths shut and play the game. And Willie played the game. I'm telling you, if Willie had stood there another second, he'd have been gone.

— 11 —

Stan Musial was the best hitter I ever saw. And Hank Aaron and Billy Williams were the only two hitters I saw who could make that bat sing. Roberto Clemente was very quiet. He never said much, but when he was at bat—if he didn't like a call—he could turn and give you a look, and everybody in the crowd immediately knew that Roberto was accusing you of kicking the call. Though he was the quietest of ballplayers, Roberto could get you in the outhouse just by looking at you.

I was there the day he got his three thousandth hit. The Pirates were playing the New York Mets at Three Rivers Stadium on September 30, 1972. Jon Matlack was pitching for the Mets, and I was the second-base umpire. After Clemente hit the ball, it went toward center field.

I was standing near second when the throw came in to the shortstop.

"Let's see it, son," I said.

He gave me the ball.

"Roberto, congratulations," I said. And I handed him the ball and shook his hand.

If I had to take a hustler, it'd be Pete Rose.

One of the joys of umpiring is getting to watch the new kids come up from the minor leagues. Sometimes a kid will come along who just impresses the hell out of you, and in spring training in 1963, Pete Rose was one of those kids.

Before a game I walked up to him and said, "Hi, pardner, how are you doing?"

"I'm Pete Rose," he said. "Who are you?"

"I'm Doug Harvey," I said, "and you can call me *umpire* or you can call me *sir*."

"Okay," he said. "I understand you."

The kid was happy-go-lucky, and he knocked our socks off the first time he walked, because on ball four he *sprinted* to first base. I knew then that Pete was different. Later, toward the end of spring training, I was umpiring his game and suddenly this kid, who had been talking his head off every minute, was standing at second base not saying a word.

"Pete, what's bothering you?" I asked him.

"Well, I don't think I'm going to make this ball club," he said. "They have so many good players."

"Shit, Pete, let me tell you something," I said. "You're not only going to make this ball club, you're going to be around for a long time."

Little did I know. I was just trying to pump the kid up, to let him know he had a chance.

"You think so?" he asked.

"I really do," I said.

Boy, he came alive, and when he hit the league he was like a breath of fresh air. He played the game the way children play the game. He played it with everything he had and put his heart into it. Pete was good for baseball, and he was good for baseball for many years.

Late in his career, Pete was playing with Montreal. My umpire crew flew there and I was bringing our bags from the airport to the ballpark, because when we went to Canada, we had to haul them ourselves. It was an off day and the other guys went home, and here it was the middle of August, hotter than hell, and I was bringing the bags in. I got the equipment man to get me a hand cart, and as I was hauling the bags out of the car I could hear this *crack, crack, crack, crack*. I couldn't understand what I was hearing. It sounded like someone was taking batting practice, even though it was an off day.

I walked into the ballpark, and on the field one of the batboys was feeding Rose pitches, and he was taking batting practice all by himself. No one worked harder at his game than Pete.

That pretty much tells you what you need to know about Pete Rose. At the time he was leading the league in hitting. He was intense, perhaps the most intense player I ever saw.

As a batter, Pete wasn't above questioning a call. And I wasn't above using my years of experience to shut him up.

Pete was playing with Philadelphia, and the Phils were playing the Mets in Philadelphia. Doc Gooden was pitching for New York. Pete came up to bat and Gooden threw a pitch, and I called a strike. Pete stepped out of the box and made a face, and suddenly sixty thousand of Philadelphia's finest were giving me the razz.

"Harv," Pete said to me, "he doesn't need any help."

I just looked at him and crossed my arms. I didn't even take my mask off.

"Come on," he said. "You're better than that. Don't let him fool you."

As Pete stepped into the box, I said to him in a low voice, "I know it missed home plate."

Pete leaped out of the box, and again the Philly throng made their feelings known.

"How come you called it a strike?" he asked.

"Well," I said, "I'm not as young as I used to be, Pete. I have a little trouble seeing now. And I guess from now on I'm going to have to call anything that's close a strike. So why don't you get back in there, and we'll see what we can do."

I wasn't above having a little fun on my own.

Doc threw another pitch, and Pete liked to have taken Gooden's head off. He ripped a single right over his right shoulder. Pete got to first base, and I took a glance over there. He had both his hands out with his palms up, explaining to the first-base coach that the pitch was *this* high.

My feeling was that Pete was good for baseball because the man loved the game. There's no doubt in my mind. He was one of the few players I can really say had fun in the game. He had as much fun playing as I had umpiring.

When Pete was chasing the National League consecutive-game hit streak record, our umpiring crew lived with him. He was hitting shots. The night the streak ended, he hit two shots, one of them at the third baseman and the other back to the pitcher. And then the other team brought in a reliever who refused to throw anything close to a strike. Pete had to chase pitches he normally wouldn't swing at, which I thought was really unfair to him. What was that pitcher going to be able to say? I stopped Pete Rose's streak? Who cares? Pete Rose was who the fans cared about.

I was there for both Hank Aaron's chase to beat Babe Ruth's career home-run record of 714 and for Pete Rose's chase to break Ty Cobb's record of 4,191 hits. It seemed that more importance was placed on Pete Rose chasing his record than Hank Aaron chasing the Babe.

Hank had finished the 1973 season one home run short of the record. The Dodgers came into Atlanta early the next season to play the Braves. The ball was jumping out of the ballpark, and on April 8, 1974, Hank hit a home run off Dodger pitcher Al Downing to break Ruth's record. He finished his career with 755 home runs.

Hank was like Clemente. They were both sullen. I understood it. Both had to fight the racism of the time. If Hank didn't agree with a call, he would have a say, but it would be under his breath and not loud. He wouldn't put on a big show. He'd just let me know that he disagreed, and that's exactly the way Clemente was.

As I said, the American public seemed more excited about Pete breaking his record than Hank breaking his. Was it racism? I don't know. I hate to think that. The game is much too big for that. To think it could be sullied because of something like that—even to kick it around, to wonder—turns my stomach a little bit.

- - -

It makes me ache me to see Pete Rose on the outside. From his play, he certainly belongs in the Hall of Fame, but he definitely broke the rules of baseball by betting on his own team. If you walk into any dressing room, you can see in red lettering the things you are forbidden from doing, and one of them is betting on baseball. Pete said he never bet against his team, but I don't give a damn. You can't bet.

Pete had a problem with gambling. He had an addiction to it. I was revulsed by the idea of it.

— 12 —

One of the great dangers of being a major league umpire is the possibility of putting yourself in a position where you can help someone win a bet on baseball. I was always very aware of that, and I made it a practice to avoid anyone who bet, who talked about betting, who wanted inside information, or anyone whom I felt might compromise my integrity. I only lost my focus one time.

In 1969 the New York Mets were scheduled to play the Atlanta Braves in the first play-off games. Everyone figured Atlanta was going to win it, because the Braves had sluggers Hank Aaron, Orlando Cepeda, and Rico Carty.

I was at home, having coffee with my folks, and my dad said to me, “I look for Atlanta to sweep the Mets.”

“What do you mean, Dad?”

“They have these boys hitting home runs,” he said.

“Dad,” I said, “let me give you a little hint: Tom Seaver, Jerry Koosman, Gary Gentry, and Nolan Ryan. These guys are outstanding pitchers, and outstanding pitchers will always beat outstanding hitters.”

It’s the reason you often have low scores in the World Series. The teams in the series most often are the ones with good pitching.

“You really think those young guys have a chance?” he asked.

“Dad,” I said, “they have a *real* good chance.”

I finished my coffee and went on my way.

After the series was over—a series the Mets won in five games—my dad came up to me and said, “I can’t thank you enough.”

“What for?”

“I had bet a hundred dollars on Atlanta to win. And when you told me about the Mets pitchers, I went and bet five hundred on the Mets.”

I was horrified.

“Jesus Christ, Dad,” I said. “This is the way I make my living. Don’t ever ask me who’s going to win.”

And he never did again.

I made it clear: My job was not to tout people.

I have to tell myself that I understand what baseball did to Pete, because baseball had warned him what it was going to do if the betting rule was violated.

And so Pete Rose, in my opinion, was the best thing that ever happened to baseball—and the worst. He deserves what he got. But I thought the world of him. Pete may get elected to the Hall of Fame when he's dead, because he has the numbers. He beat Ty Cobb's hit record. He was one of the greats.

CHAPTER 12

JOCKO AND SHAG

—1—

Toward the end of my second year in the big leagues, *Sports Illustrated* wrote an article in which it voted me the outstanding umpire in the National League. Al Barlick was spitting nickels, believe me. It was tough for him to take. And tough for a lot of the other veteran umpires as well.

Oh, did Barlick try to bury me. I went to the guy who wrote the article and pleaded with him, "Please, whatever you do, don't ever do this again. You've gotten me buried."

Fortunately for me, after two years of being tortured by Al Barlick, I was transferred to Jocko Conlan's crew for the 1964 season. Jocko was a little guy, feisty, and he'd fight at the drop of a hat. He was a presence, which is a central theme when you talk about the great ones.

Jocko Conlan was an ex-ballplayer. He had played outfield for the Chicago White Sox, and after his playing days were over, he used to work the high steel in Chicago.

One day he was up on a tall skyscraper, and he said it was colder than shit. He just couldn't believe how cold it was, and he was having trouble hanging on to the steel.

"Fuck this," he said, and as he rode down he told himself, *I'm going someplace where the sun shines.*

He headed for Arizona, and when he arrived, the Cubs were playing the St. Louis Browns. When umpire Red Ormsby fell ill because of the heat, Jocko was asked if he would fill in.

"Jocko," they said, "we won't give you any shit."

He went out, fell in love with it, and asked if he could get a job umpiring in the minor leagues. The next year he was umpiring in the minors. His major league umpiring career began in 1941, and I was part of his crew when he retired in 1965.

His most famous argument was with Leo Durocher. Leo was kicking dirt and accidentally kicked Jocko in the shins. Jocko, angered, kicked Leo in the shins. Jocko, the plate umpire, was wearing shin guards. Leo wasn't.

Afterward Leo was heard to say, "You guys are wearing shin guards. What the fuck was I doing?"

Jocko was a sweetheart. I loved working with him. Jocko could charm anyone. He always had the writers around him, and that just pissed off Al Barlick. Jocko and Al hated each other. Jocko could make friends with anybody and Al couldn't. Al always said Jocko made it to the Hall of Fame because of all the sportswriters he befriended. That's not fair. Jocko was an excellent umpire, and of course he was behind the plate when Don Larsen pitched his perfect game. That didn't hurt.

Jocko was the funniest guy I ever umpired with. One time we were in Milwaukee when a beach ball went bouncing out past second base. Jocko was umpiring at second. Jocko ran over and grabbed the ball, which he stuck under his arm like it was a football. He went running off the field, putting out his left arm like he was going to straight-arm someone.

He wasn't quite so funny when it came to getting the game started on time. Jocko was a stickler for making sure that if the game was supposed to start at 1:05, it didn't start a minute later.

A music group was scheduled to play between games of a doubleheader in Milwaukee, and as a group of roadies came out onto the field and began setting up the instruments, Jocko went over to the general manager and warned him he better get the band off the field by the time the second game was supposed to start.

"Don't worry," said the GM. "We'll be out of here."

The umpires went back to our dressing room, and when the time came for us to start the second game, the group was still playing their World War II songs.

"Hey," said Jocko to the general manager, "I told you I wanted these guys out of here when I came out."

"Jocko," the GM said, "this is their last song."

"They just did their last song," said Jocko, and he took his foot and kicked down the front row of stands on which the band was playing.

"Now get the hell off the stage," he said.

— 2 —

Toward the end of his career, Jocko developed a serious drinking problem. He liked his toddies. He'd buy me a drink and I'd buy him two drinks. One year I had to work three plate jobs for him because he came down from his hotel room drunk, and we left him back at the hotel. I didn't hold that against him. He was in his last year in the league, and it was hotter'n hell, so what was wrong with giving the old man a day off? That's just the way I felt about him. Tony Venzon wasn't quite so generous.

"I'm not working your fucking plate," was what Tony told him. "You either show up, or it's not going to get worked."

After he said that, I had a talk with Lee Weyer, and Lee was also willing to work the plate in Jocko's absence. Lee didn't mind either.

His last year in the league, Jocko went out singing. Jocko and I would go to a bar—in Chicago there was a bar one block directly behind our hotel—and if it was a day game, he'd spend the evening drinking.

Jocko and I would sing a lot together. We had a lot of fun.

Jocko, who died in 1989, was very ill and in the hospital. Joy and I went and saw him. He had his gown on and we were walking down the aisle singing, "When your old wedding ring was new / and the love in your heart was true / I remember with pride as we stood side by side /what a beautiful picture you made as my bride."

— 3 —

After Jocko retired, I became a member of Shag Crawford's umpiring crew. I was with Shag for the next twelve years. Shag and I had similar upbringings. We came from poor backgrounds. Before he became an umpire, he drove a milk truck. He was a catcher in the Philadelphia A's farm system but hurt his arm and wasn't able to play, and he began umpiring in the sandlots. Johnny Stevens, an umpire from the Philadelphia area, saw him and recommended him. Like me, he never went to umpire school.

Shag was the best umpire I ever worked with. He had a great feel for the game and for his fellow umpires.

Shag was a real man and all Irish. He was a tough guy. A newspaperman would come into our locker room after a game and ask Shag a question like, "You're the one who ejected him? Why did you do it?"

Shag would blow his Irish stack and call the guy every motherfucker in the world.

"Get the fuck out of here before I kill you," he'd say.

This was when newspaper writers were electing the members of the Hall of Fame, and I do think it's what kept him out.

Over the years, Shag and I had some hellacious arguments. I can recall a flight from Los Angeles to Chicago. I don't sleep on night flights, so I was talking to another member of our crew, Johnny Kibler, all the way to Chicago.

We were talking about umpiring. Shag was sitting there on the plane, drinking, until it finally put him to sleep.

When we got off the plane Shag was still a bit buzzed, and John and I were still talking baseball.

Shag attacked me, really jumped on my ass.

"What the fuck are you trying to do, take over my crew?" he asked.

"No, Shag," I said. "God almighty, I would never do that."

"I hear you talking to him," he said. "I'll tell you one thing. You better not be trying it anymore, because I'll send you to help someone else. I don't need you on my crew."

"Okay, Shag."

The next day I was walking around downtown Chicago before we were to leave for the ballpark. It was about ten in the morning. I had had breakfast, and I heard "Yo." I looked across the street and it was Shag. He was waving for me to come over. I didn't know whether he was still pissed; whether he wanted to take a swing at me.

But don't get me wrong. I loved the guy. I dearly loved him. And here's the reason: He called me over and so I went, still on the alert, and walked over to him.

He pointed to a pair of shoes in the window of a shoe store.

"What do you think of those?" he asked. "Are those me?"

"No," I said, "not unless you're going gay."

"I didn't think so," he said. "Come on. Let's go, kid."

And that was the end of the argument.

The great thing with Shag was when it was over, it was over. He never held a grudge as far as we were concerned. Shag could get mad at me, but we could always settle it.

— 4 —

Another aspect of Shag's personality that I greatly admired was that he was always fair. I would find out that wasn't necessarily true of all crew chiefs. During the time I was working under Shag, I was asked to join Tom Gorman's crew for one three-game series. They were down a man and they decided to send me to Gorman, because they had umpired a tough series and they wanted to send a young umpire to go on Shag Crawford's crew for a few days.

When I arrived in Atlanta, Gorman asked me, "Where did you work last night?" I told him I had worked the plate. Ordinarily when you leave one crew and go to another, you are assigned third base. It's what Al Barlick or Shag Crawford would have done. Had Gorman done that, I wouldn't have had to work home plate during the three-game series. But Tom told me to go to second base, and so for game three I had the plate.

After I returned to Shag's crew, Shag said to me, "Harv, I watched the game on TV. Did that son of a bitch put you at second base?"

"Yeah, he did, Shag," I said.

"That Irish cocksucker," said Shag.

Here was one Irishman calling another one a cocksucker, and that was all right.

During that series I lost a lot of respect for Tom Gorman for another reason. Al Forman was behind the plate on this day, and he and Pittsburgh manager Danny Murtaugh began arguing. Gorman and I walked over so we could be witnesses to whatever was going on.

As Gorman was walking toward him, Murtaugh turned around and said to him, "You get your fat ass back where you belong. I don't want to fucking talk to you at all."

"Calm down, Danny," Gorman said to him.

Gorman not only didn't eject Murtaugh, he took it and kept quiet.

I turned and walked away. I could only shake my head when he didn't eject Murtaugh. Al Barlick taught me that they were to call us *sir* or *Mr. Umpire*, and if they called us anything else, we were to eject them.

— 5 —

In my early years of umpiring all three of my crew chiefs—Al Barlick, Jocko Conlan, and Shag Crawford—drank heavily. And I would drink along with them, though I was a terrible drinker.

When I was a boy, I was the batboy for the El Centro Imperials, and I can remember making deliveries to the umpires at their hotel. They were staying in a second-rate hotel in town, and the rooms didn't have air-conditioning. All they had was a fan at the end of the hallway. You could open the transom to your room and the fan would blow some air around to cool you off a little, but not much. It was usually over 100 degrees in the summer. The fan was just moving the air. It was so hot the umpires couldn't stay in their rooms during the evening. There was nothing to do and they had to get out of their rooms, so they went to the hotel bar and drank. You sat in the bar and sipped cold beer. And if you left the bartender a couple of tickets, many times he would pick up the tab. That's where it came from. The guys all learned to drink in the minor leagues.

When I became an umpire in the minor leagues, there wasn't a whole lot to do except go to the hotel bar, bullshit the evening away, and drink. It's what you did. You got trapped into it.

About five years into my career, one day I realized that I had become a drunken bum. I finally realized that when you're drinking and drinking hard, no one is going to stop you but yourself. I'd go out and get loaded with the guys, and half the time I'd wake up in the morning with my clothes still on. I finally said to myself, *God almighty, what am I doing?*

I finally said, *This is freaking ridiculous.*

There was another reason I was drinking so much in the major leagues. For the first time in my life, I had the money to do it. You have to remember: In the minor leagues you're making so little money that you're almost starving to death. Your wife has to work. You're trying to pay your bills with what little money you've got.

Then all of a sudden you go to the major leagues and you've got a decent per diem—which you never had before—and you have more money than you know what to do with. You always ride with your partners in the cabs, and even as a first-year umpire I could see that we always got a deal at the hotels. We'd leave tickets to the game with the hotel managers, and they'd give us a really good deal for the rooms. With the money you had left, you could get drunk every night.

The first three and a half or four years, I drank too much. I realized it when I was going home. I was drunk calling my wife at home, and it couldn't have been any fun. Later I asked her about it and she said it was terrible. So I did a good thing. I quit drinking, except once every two weeks or so, I'd have a glass of wine with my partners to let them know I still loved them.

After that, I put all of that energy into my umpiring, because I'm not a chaser. I told my wife when I asked her to be my bride, "I've chased all the women I want to chase. You're the woman I want to be married to." And I kept my promise to her. It'll be fifty-three years this year.

CHAPTER 13

MEMORABLE MOMENTS

— 1 —

Don't let anybody tell you that baseball isn't a violent game. I've seen players slide into a base trying to cut a player's leg. And I was behind the plate when Dickie Thon was hit in the head with a pitch that almost blew out his eyeball.

I was behind the plate that day in the Astrodome. Mike Torrez was pitching for the Mets, and he threw a pitch on the outside part of the plate and I called it a strike. Dickie had moved closer to the plate to be able to reach that pitch. The next pitch sailed right at his head and smashed into his face. It was terrible.

Mike Torrez was broken up by it. He hadn't meant to hit him. The ball just sailed, and I put that in my report. Dickie missed the entire season, and it took him a while before he could play again.

I also saw some nasty street fights in front of home plate that made me sick to my stomach.

— 2 —

Juan Marichal, the San Francisco Giants' Hall of Fame pitcher, gave me the worst moment of my career. Because of the way he pitched, Juan was very tough with umpires behind the plate. He threw the ball from four different places: overhand, three-quarters, side-arm, and underhand, and you never knew what was coming. He had a great changeup and a moving fastball that he could move six to eight inches from left to right. The whole time he was in the league I never had a run-in with him. With the great ones, you never do.

I was umpiring at third that day. Marichal was batting. The first pitch was a strike. When Roseboro threw the ball back to the mound, the throw grazed Marichal's ear. I could see Marichal turn around and say something to Roseboro. Herman Franks, the Giants' manager, said all Marichal said to Roseboro was, "Why did you do that?"

Then after the next pitch, Roseboro started to get up out

of his crouch and take a step toward Marichal, and before anyone could stop him, Marichal raised his bat with one hand and cracked Roseboro over the head with a sickening *thud.* Blood poured from an open wound in Roseboro's head.

Willie Mays, always a peacemaker, rushed over to Roseboro, perhaps his best friend in baseball, and cradled his head. Mays's uniform was splattered with Roseboro's blood. Mays placed his head on Roseboro's chest and cried, "Johnny, Johnny, I'm so sorry."

Shag Crawford, who was umpiring behind the plate, tackled the crazed Marichal to keep him from doing further damage. When I saw this, I ran in as a peacemaker, and all of a sudden there was a mass of humanity all in a pile around home plate. Don Drysdale, a big man, was the first out of the Dodger dugout. He ran past me as I was running to try to protect Shag.

I jumped on the pile, digging down, trying to get to Shag and hollering his name, and I could hear Dodger pitcher Howie Reed, who was down at the bottom, yelling, "I've got him. I've got him."

Reed had a hold of one of Marichal's legs, and Marichal was ripping Reed's uniform to shreds, kicking with his other cleat.

"Turn him loose, you damn fool," I said to Reed. "Get out of here. Look at your chest."

He was covered with blood.

I never did find Shag until the pile was broken up and order was restored.

Marichal was escorted off the field, and Roseboro also had to leave, a red-stained towel pressed against his head.

The police came down to the field, and the next afternoon when we came to the ballpark, Shag called the head of police and ripped him a new asshole for going onto the field.

"Don't you ever come out here," Shag said. "This is our bailiwick. We'll handle it. If I ever see you out here again, I'll report you, and I'll do everything I can to get your job."

Later there was a hearing. Marichal said under oath that when Roseboro threw the ball back, he threw it right next to his ear, and the second time, he said he actually ticked his ear. For that he clubbed him over the head with his bat.

Roseboro was hurt badly. Marichal was fined and had to miss a turn.

I was called on to testify the next season. When I was asked, "Who was pitching against Marichal?" I said, "I don't know." I didn't remember. Turns out it was Sandy Koufax, in one of only three times Koufax and Marichal ever faced each other. I simply forgot, and I told them, "Let me get something straight with you. When I walk off the field, unless I have a report to write, what's over and done with is over and done with. I wash it from my mind."

The only other time I saw a player throw a bat occurred in a game in which Bob Gibson pitched. Gibson drilled the batter deliberately because he had hit a home run, and the next time Gibson came to bat, the pitcher drilled him. Gibson was really pissed, so he threw his bat at the guy. I then ejected Gibson, and Gibson was mad at me. He was always mad at someone.

— 3 —

When a young catcher comes up to the big leagues, I tell him, "Young man, let me tell you something. My name is Mr. Harvey. My name is *sir*. My name is *ump*. You can call me by any of those three names, and we'll get along just fine.

"Remember one thing: Umpires are trying their best to get everything right, and it's impossible."

Basically I tell them: "If you keep your mouth shut, you will get along with the umpires just fine."

As you can see, more than anything, umpires are looking for respect. We aren't asking for it. We're demanding it.

I umpired my first World Series in 1968, and before the first game, commissioner William Eckert's right-hand man, Joe Reichler, met with the umpiring crew. He wanted to let us know how the series was going to be run.

"At no time will we have any ejections of ballplayers," he said. "The people are here to see them play."

The other umpires had more seniority than I did, and none of them said a word. I looked over at Bill Haller and he looked back at me. I was hoping Bill would speak up, but when he didn't, I raised my hand.

"Do you have something to add?" asked Reichler.

"I sure do," I said. "It's taken me seven years to get here, and during that time I have been teaching the players what they can and cannot call me, and I'm telling you right now, if one of them calls me a son of a bitch or a cocksucker, I'm going to unload him. If you don't like that, you better get somebody else to umpire these ball games for you, because I'm not going to be here."

That's the way I looked at baseball, because that was the way I was taught by Al Barlick.

He jumped right over it.

"Well," said Reichler, "let's get on to the next order of business."

But that's the way I felt. It took me long enough to teach the players that nobody calls me a son of a bitch and stays in a ball game, and I wasn't going to let Joe Reichler, General Eckert, or anyone else take that away from me.

As it turned out, we didn't have to run anyone. It was the World Series, and the players were on their best behavior. You don't get many complaints during the World Series.

— 4 —

Every umpire goes about his business believing he's always right, even when he knows he isn't. That's part of being a good umpire. Being involved in controversial calls is also part of being an umpire. In my case, my most controversial call occurred in the fifth game of the 1968 World Series between the St. Louis Cardinals and the Detroit Tigers when I called Lou Brock out at the plate on a very close play.

One of the highlights of the day was the singing of the National Anthem, sung by that blind guy, José Feliciano. He accompanied himself on the guitar, and in his rendition he sang so slowly I didn't think he'd ever finish. He also sang it as a dirge. When he was done, a lot of the fans booed him. But no one ever forgot it.

The Tigers ended up winning the game and the series. Whenever I see Brock, he's quick to remind me that I cost him $13,000, the difference between the winners' and losers' share.

After the game we had to run like hell to catch our charter flight, since we were flying back to St. Louis. I was all worked up, sweating like a pig, so I took a quick shower, headed for the airport, and got on the plane.

In my seat I ordered a beer and sat there relaxing with my wife.

Baseball commissioner Eckert kept the plane waiting for forty-five minutes. I watched as he came charging on. Joe Reichler was with him. Reichler came over to my seat to see me. He began pounding on my shoulders to get my attention, and he was screaming "Harvey, Harvey" loud enough that he could have been using a bullhorn.

I looked up to see him looming over me.

"Harvey, Harvey," Reichler said. "They can't prove you wrong. We just spent a half hour reviewing the film of the Brock play at the plate, and they can't prove you wrong.

"Try as we might," he continued, "we couldn't find anything wrong with your call. You got it right."

Hell, I knew I had the play right.

My blood started to boil.

"Why the fuck are you trying to prove me wrong in the first place?" I said. "Now get the fuck away from me. Don't come to me and tell me they couldn't prove me wrong."

I then felt like an idiot because my wife and Edna Stengel were sitting right across the aisle from me, and I don't usually curse in front of my wife. I apologized to the ladies, and everyone around me gave me a hand.

Over the years I'd run into Lou Brock, and he'd say to me, "You cost me a lot of money."

He still talks about that.

— 5 —

One of the worst days of my umpiring life came in Houston. I was umpiring behind the plate, and we walked out to home plate and took the lineup cards from the managers. I looked down to the bullpens where the starting pitchers were warming up. There in Houston's bullpen was Joe Niekro, and when I looked down to the Braves bullpen, there was Phil Niekro. I had two knuckleballers to work, and catching a knuckleball is like trying to catch a gnat with a pair of tweezers. Umpiring a knuckleballer is just as bad as catching one. And in this game I had two of them pitching.

If you don't wait for that ball to hit the glove, chances are good you're going to kick the call, because the ball moves the most when it slows down.

Phil Niekro threw the greatest knuckleball I ever saw. We were in Atlanta—the Braves against Cincinnati. Tony Cloninger, the only pitcher ever to hit two grand-slam home runs in a game, was pitching for the Reds. The bases were loaded and Niekro had two strikes on the big pitcher, and he threw a knuckler.

The catcher leaped out to the right, and just as he leaped it was like the ball hit a magic wall. It came straight across and crossed home plate and hit me in the left shoulder and dropped down. The pitch was in the strike zone, so it was strike three, and Cloninger took off running.

The bases were loaded. The Atlanta catcher had enough sense to grab the ball and run over and step on home plate—a force-out.

But that was the greatest knuckleball I had ever seen, thrown by Phil Niekro.

— 6 —

The umpires in both the American and National Leagues formed a union in 1963, my second year in the league. Our pay was terrible. For my first few years my pay was $8,000 a year. We had no benefits and our pension was a joke. Our retirement pay was a crummy hundred dollars a year for every year of service. So after umpiring in major league baseball for thirty years, your retirement pay would be $3,000 a year. You can't live on that.

I was willing to stand up and tell them they were wrong.

For years it was all Joy and I could do to keep from starving to death. It seemed that the umpires were always at the bottom of the pot. Everyone else got taken care of before they got to us. Major League Baseball didn't really want to pay for integrity, hard work, or all that travel.

Today an umpire can make as much as $200,000 a year, but it was our organizing that got it all started. I'm proud to say I was a signer of the original charter for the umpires union. It was my second year and we met in Chicago. Mel Steiner came over to me and said, "Harvey, what the fuck are you doing here?"

"Beg your pardon?" I said.

"You're a two-year man," said Steiner. "Are you sure you want to stick your neck into this?"

"Let me tell you something, Mel," I said. "I believe in what they're doing and I'm standing up for it. If I lose my job, I'll get back on a truck next week."

It was the attitude I took, because I knew something had to be done: The pay was terrible. In the American League the umpires were getting pension payments of $150 a year, because American League president Joe Cronin had given them a $50-a-year raise to keep them working. When that happened the American League umpires stopped going to our union meetings. When we hired a lawyer to represent us, only the National League umpires were paying him.

In 1970 we went on strike. By gosh, sixteen men went out, and it took a lot of guts to do it. Joy and I talked it over, and we agreed: We had nothing to lose because we were at the bottom of the pile. If we won, we'd have a chance for things to be better, and if we lost and I didn't have a job, I would find another one in an instant.

I had always worked, and I'd just get another job and go on with my life.

Our first work stoppage took place back east in Pittsburgh. We put up a picket line at each entrance of the stadium. Pittsburgh is a great union town, which was the reason we did it there. Fans who had purchased tickets would come up to us and ask what was going on, and after we told them, they would rip up their tickets and go home. We could see they had strong union sentiments.

The electricians told management, "If the pickets set up before we get to the park, we will honor their picket line." That meant there'd be no lights, and so management went out and brought in four giant generators to power the lights.

But when they came to turn on the generators, they found signs that said *Danger. Explosives. Don't touch*.

A close friend of mine, Joey Diven, a union guy who had a hundred roles in a strong union city—a guy involved in politics who knew everyone—had put up the signs, making management wonder what would happen if they started up the generators.

After a one-day strike, Major League Baseball agreed to give us a much better per diem.

— 7 —

The next improvement we wanted was to get hospitalization. We didn't have it when our two sons were born. I didn't have it when Bob Gibson knocked out my two teeth in Pittsburgh and my gums became infected. Finally, we got hospitalization.

Why Major League Baseball always took a hard line against us was always a mystery. It was asinine. They could have settled the whole thing for cheaper than what they had to go through.

We struck for a day during the 1970 play-offs. All the umpires—this time National and American—went out. We were in the middle of negotiations and we weren't getting anywhere. We felt we had no choice.

One time we went on strike, and baseball hired scabs and gave them five-year contracts. Meanwhile, we were getting only one-year contracts, and the league had the right to fire you at will. You know how it is with management and workers. You always hate your boss. But Joy would always say to me, "If you're one of the best umpires, why are you treated so badly?"

It was only after Richie Phillips took over the union in 1978 that we got a decent salary and a modicum of respect. For many years before that we felt we got very little respect from anyone, including the baseball people in the league office.

In the beginning it was, "You're lucky to have a job." In fact, during one of our strikes, Joe Cronin, the American League president, said, "We could just go out and get a bunch of garbage-truck drivers to replace these people." *These people* were the striking umpires.

With Richie Phillips's help, Joy wrote a letter to the *Los Angeles Times* in rebuttal. She wrote that every job has a measure of respect to it, including garbage-truck drivers, and for Cronin to try to denigrate one trade with another showed a great lack of respect for the work ethic of the American people.

Everyone has a job to do—and apparently everyone thinks your job is easier than his.

CHAPTER 14

CREW CHIEF

— 1 —

Baseball made me a crew chief in 1977, choosing me over two other umpires with more seniority, Paul Pryor and John McSherry. The league in the past had always assigned crew chiefs according to how much time they had served. Not this time. And Paul and John were both assigned to my crew, which I thought was an unfairness. It was as though the executives in charge of the umpires wanted to make my life as difficult as possible.

I took each of them aside.

"It was none of my doing," I said. "I'm not an ass-kisser. I didn't ask to be crew chief. It was handed to me, and I'm going to take it. If you want to be on my crew, that's fine. If you don't, I'm sure I can arrange to have you transferred."

Both Paul and John accepted it, and we had a fine year. There wasn't a single problem that we couldn't handle.

Paul was a fine fellow and a very decent umpire. He did have one problem. Like so many others, he drank too much. His favorite drink was whiskey.

Paul's problem surfaced in Pittsburgh. I was staying at a different hotel from my crew members. They liked to stay downtown, where the action was. I preferred quiet. I stayed at the Holiday Inn, about eight blocks from Forbes Field. I liked to stay there because I could walk to the park.

On this day I arrived early. The equipment man was in the locker room. He was hanging up our clothes for the game.

"Harvey, can I have a word with you?" he asked.

"Certainly."

"Paul Pryor's drinking so much," he said, "that after a game when he's working home plate, his uniform is soaked with sweat and it stinks something terrible. I'd wash it, but I can't do that. It has to be dry-cleaned. Can you talk to him?"

I went to Paul and told him, "It stinks to high heaven."

"Okay, Harv," Paul said, "I'll quit drinking whiskey."

And he did, though he did switch to vodka, which wasn't quite so bad.

John McSherry, a large man who weighed more than three hundred pounds, was a good fellow and a very good umpire. He not only had a drinking problem, he had an eating problem. On an off day during spring training I went to see him in his hotel room. When I walked in, he was lying in bed watching TV. Beside him was a case of Pepsi-Cola and an ice bucket. He was eating a full meal. It was ten o'clock in the morning. It was clear to me he had an eating habit he just couldn't break.

Later John was promoted to crew chief. He was umpiring behind the plate on opening day in Cincinnati in 1996. He started to walk off, took a few steps, and collapsed and died.

Eric Gregg, who was on my crew and was the best of the African American umpires, also had a terrible problem with food. I was forever on Eric about it. Had he listened to me, he'd still be alive.

Eric was an outstanding umpire, but his weight became a problem. He could hardly move. There are pictures of him trying to work behind home plate. He had his legs spread out as far as he could get them because he couldn't bend down.

One time Frank Pulli and Jerry Crawford, the other members of my crew, came to me and asked if on a certain play where Eric was supposed to run out to the outfield, one of them could come out instead and cover for him.

I told them no. I was hoping to force Eric to fix his eating problem.

One time after a night game our crew was invited out to dinner. Eric said he couldn't go, he had something to do. The three of us went out to dinner and stayed out late, returning at about one thirty in the morning. We were walking to our hotel rooms when we saw the bellman pushing a big tray.

"Hold it, partner," I said to him. We looked under the tray, and there was a slab of ribs, a whole chicken, and four beers.

"Are you going to Eric Gregg's room?" I asked him.

"Yeah," he said.

I gave the guy ten bucks and took one of my cards and wrote Eric a note.

Enjoy your snack, I wrote, and I put it on the tray.

We stood out by Eric's door. The bellman left the tray and exited, tossing a baseball up and down. Eric had given it to him as a tip.

Two minutes later the door opened and the tray came flying out. Eric, caught red-handed stuffing his face at one thirty in the morning, had thrown everything on the tray out the hotel window into the parking lot.

I loved Eric. I thought the world of him. He was fun. Eric was sure he was bulletproof as far as his job security.

"Because of my color," he told me, "I'll always be here. I'll be the one they keep."

He was wrong. After the umpires went on strike in 1992, they kept Charlie Williams, the other African American umpire, and they let Eric go. It broke his heart. Broke mine too.

Another of the umpires who worked on my crew was Dick Stello, a really terrific guy. Everyone loved him. Dick was a lot of fun, a good guy. He was married to Lillian, who at one time had worked as an exotic dancer under the name of Chesty Morgan. We called her Zsa Zsa; a nice lady. He would tell us about some of the things she'd do, and we'd laugh. When they were married,

Dick was her manager. After they divorced, they still remained close. He loved bling. He had a big watch and chain and always had jewelry around his neck.

Dick was killed in a freak car accident in November 1987. He and Lillian lived in St. Petersburg, Florida, and after buying a classic car at a car auction he needed to put a license plate on it. He pulled over to the side of the road and was putting on the tag when a car came out of nowhere and hit him and crushed him. It was awful.

Dick is really missed. It was a shame.

In all, I was crew chief between 1974 and 1992, and I wouldn't have traded a minute of it.

The Cincinnati Reds, featuring Pete Rose, Johnny Bench, Bernie Carbo, Bobby Tolan, and Tony Pérez, among others, won 102 ball games in 1970. The Reds' manager was Sparky Anderson.

You had to be careful with Sparky. Sparky always tried to put the hat on you. He'd try to get you to say something he could use against you. If you got flustered and got to talking too fast, you might say something where he'd say, "Wait a minute. You said . . ." And you couldn't deny it, because you said it.

And Sparky, unlike most managers, prided himself on knowing the rules. Well, Sparky didn't know them compared to Doug Harvey. There were times I would listen to Sparky talk, then I'd tell him, "You're wrong, Sparky."

"What do you mean?"

"What you're trying to spout is rule so-and-so, and you're spouting it wrong."

I would put him down, and he'd just stomp off upset.

Sparky was a good manager. He enjoyed a good argument, but many times he didn't heed my rule about calling me *sir* or *Mr. Umpire* or *Mr. Harvey,* and Sparky'd get ejected for being disrespectful.

Sparky's Reds were playing the San Francisco Giants. I was at second base and Jerry Crawford was at first. Bill Plummer, the Reds' catcher, was at bat. He had two strikes on him and he checked his swing. The plate umpire, Andy Olsen, nodded to Jerry, and he rang Plummer up.

Plummer raised his arms and yelled at Jerry, and Jerry threw him out.

Sparky came out of the dugout on a dead run.

"Son, I don't think you like Bill Plummer," he said to Jerry. "It's the second time you've ejected him this year."

Sparky had his finger out, pointing, giving Jerry a lecture.

"Sparky," said Jerry, "I don't have anything against Plummer. All he had to do was keep his mouth shut, and everything would have been all right."

The Reds took the field. A Giant base runner went to steal second. The throw from the catcher went to Reds shortstop Dave Concepción, who caught the ball, brought it down, and tagged the runner. I called him safe. He had slid under the tag.

Here comes Sparky on a dead run. We argued pretty good, though I never raised my voice. One of the things Sparky said to me was, "The reason you called him safe was to get the team off Crawford's ass."

I was furious. That he would think I would cheat just to get the crowd off another umpire's butt was insulting and infuriating.

When Sparky walked away he turned to Dave Concepción and patted his belly.

"No guts," he said, pointing, talking about me.

Sparky was better than halfway to the dugout, and I took to running after him. He was in the habit of jumping over the foul line, and I caught him in the middle of his jump. I nailed him in the shoulder and almost knocked him down.

"Get the fuck out of here, and don't you say one word," I said. "I'll show you guts. One way or another I'll pick everyone off your ball club and throw them out. Now get out of here."

And he did.

About six weeks later we were in Cincinnati, and Dave Concepción came into our dressing room to inform me that the Reds ball club had voted it the ejection of the century.

"That was the greatest ejection we ever saw," he said.

I laughed like hell over that.

— 2 —

I was involved in two World Series between the Dodgers and Oakland. I was behind the plate in 1988 when Kirk Gibson hit his dramatic home run off Dennis Eckersley. As a baseball purist who always hated it when the game wasn't played right, I was upset because Mike Davis, who got on before Kirk, stole second to put the tying run in scoring position, and the A's didn't even try to make a play on him. Now a bloop single would score him. I understand the fielders had a lot of confidence in Eckersley, but damn, I was mad at that. And then the big guy, Gibson, came up to bat.

Oh no, not him, everyone rooting for the Dodgers was moaning. Gibson was badly hurt. He wasn't expected to play. How could he even swing the bat? But then he swung, letting loose of the bat with his back hand. It's why I was watching the ball wondering, *My God, can that get out?*

When I saw the ball go up in the air, my impression was that it would either be a home run or it would be caught. It landed in the seats—one of the greatest home runs in World Series history, especially after Gibson gimped around the bases pumping his arm. As he limped around the diamond I was wondering, *Is he going to fall down on the base paths?*

The Los Angeles media voted it the most exciting sports event ever to take place there.

— 3 —

Earlier in the Kirk Gibson home-run game there was a man on first when Dave Parker hit a ball that went straight into the ground. He took off running. Mike Scioscia, the Dodgers' catcher, came out, picked it up, and threw to first, hitting Parker. The ball rolled into right field, and as Parker barreled around first and into second base, I was yelling, "Time-out. Time-out." But nobody saw or heard me.

Parker wasn't in the first-base running lane, and if a runner is hit by a throw while running outside the lane, he's out. I went over to Parker to explain that he was out, and I told the runner who had been on first that he had to go back.

The A's manager, Tony La Russa, came out to ask what had happened. I explained that the ball had just touched the top of Parker's head, and that when I looked down, he was running inside the first-base lane.

"Now, Harv, that's not true," said La Russa. "Let me say something."

"Go right ahead," I replied.

"I was sitting over there. And I was watching that ball when it was thrown. And I could see it. It didn't hit him."

It dawned on me that I was talking to a lawyer. La Russa, a pretty bright guy, has a law degree. So I decided to put things in legal terms that he could understand.

"Let me present my case," I said.

He looked at me funny, then said, "All right."

"If I really thought I could see those plays better from over there," I said, "I'd sit right next to you."

End of argument.

— 4 —

After the game Oakland general manager Sandy Alderson was bitching and moaning because the batter before Kirk Gibson homered had walked on a 3-2 count, and Alderson made the statement, "If Harvey had called the last pitch a strike instead of a ball, Gibson never would have gotten up."

I was really pissed, because he was accusing me of missing the pitch. I went back and reviewed the film, and the pitch was about six inches off the plate. It wasn't even close. Alderson said it should have been called a strike. Screw him.

After Gibson hit that home run, the series was as good as over: Oakland wasn't the same ball club, and Eckersley never got into another game. Orel Hershiser was masterful in game five. He just stuck Oakland's bats right up their noses. They didn't stand a chance.

— 5 —

It was announced before the end of the 1975 season that I would be one of the umpires for the World Series, which was between the Boston Red Sox and the Cincinnati Reds. I was walking across the hotel lobby at one in the morning.

I heard someone say, "Mr. Harvey."

I turned around and it was Carl Yastrzemski, the talented Red Sox outfielder.

We talked for a few minutes, and Carl said, "Oh, we've all heard about you. We're all anxious when we get to the World Series that you might work the plate. The guys really know all about you and have a lot of respect for you."

What is this American Leaguer telling me this for? I thought.

I found it interesting and I was touched.

— 6 —

The game in which I was given the nickname "God" was played in the evening in New York, and it was raining. The night before Frank Cashen, the Mets' general manager, called down to our dressing room and said, "Tomorrow it's supposed to rain, and also the next day. Tomorrow we'll be lucky to get the game in, and the next day no chance, and it's their last trip here. It means we have to play a doubleheader in their ballpark in San Diego. I'd appreciate it if you could get the game in tonight."

"I work hard to get every game in," I told him. "If it can be played at all, I will get it in."

"Thank you," Cashen said. "That's all I can ask."

All the grounds crews had a certain affinity for us, because when they saw Harvey's crew coming and there was a potential rain situation, they would tell all the members of the grounds crew, "You guys better get your rain gear on, because we're going to work today. Harvey's here, and he doesn't give up games."

I'd rather fight the rain in the cool weather than to lose the game and have a doubleheader in the hot weather.

The next day I had the plate. I was working my butt off and it was raining lightly. My rule always was that I would allow the game to continue until it became unsafe. Of course, I was also trying to get in four and a half innings so the game would be official and count.

I got in six innings. There was no score and there were two outs. Mookie Wilson hit a ground ball to Steve Garvey at first base. Before the slowly hit ball even got to him, Steve held up his hand to tell the pitcher he had the play under control. Garvey fielded the ball, then took one step and his legs flew out from under him. Wilson was safe at first.

Clearly it wasn't safe to continue. I called time and ruled there would be a game delay. I ordered the grounds crew to repair the area around first base and cover the infield. After a while the rain let up, and I ordered the game to continue.

Mookie was on first base with two outs, and Darryl Strawberry, the big outfielder for the Mets, got up and hit the ball four miles. At the end of the sixth inning, the Mets had a 2–0 lead. We had just started the next inning when the rain began coming down hard. I had the grounds crew cover the infield.

I was soaked, and I told Joe West, who was part of my umpiring crew, "Stay out here. I'm going to go in and change my underwear. Let me know if it stops raining."

Not too long afterward Joe came into our dressing room, laughing. You have to hear his country-boy laugh. He's got a wide-open laugh, and I love him. So Joe was laughing, *ha-ha-ha-ha-ha*.

"What's so funny, Joe?" I asked.

He was laughing so hard he could barely tell me.

"I went over and sat in the San Diego dugout," he said.

"Why'd you do that?" I asked. "They're losing, and they're the ones who are going to be upset."

"Aw, hell," he said, "I figured I'd do that. Anyway, Garvey comes in, and he said to me, 'Didn't anybody check the infield?'

"'Yeah,' I said. 'Chief checked it.'

"And down at the other end of the dugout Terry Kennedy was taking off his catcher's gear, and he slammed his shin guards down on the bench and said, 'Well, that does it. Because that son of a bitch walks on water.'"

West thought it was the funniest thing he'd ever heard, and he told the story to *Chicago Tribune* sportswriter Jerome

Holtzman. I liked Jerry. We trusted him. He wrote what you told him.

The next trip to Chicago, I checked the field to make sure it was all right, which I did every time, and I came into our dressing room. One of my crew said, "Jerry Holtzman was here."

"I'm sorry I missed him," I said.

The next morning the headline of Jerry's column was GOD VISITS CHICAGO.

He was talking about me.

That morning the other members of my crew and I got into a cab. We were headed for the ballpark, and Jerry Crawford said, "Hey, chief, we thought you'd like to see this."

That's how I learned of it.

"My God," I said.

"No," they said, "*you're* the God."

After that, everyone started referring to me as "God."

Every time Lenny Dykstra, who was playing center field for the Philadelphia Phillies, would run into me—no matter where I was on the field, even if I was at third base and he was in the right-field dugout—he would come running by me on the way to his position and say, "Hello, God." Lenny thought that was the greatest thing in the world.

How did I feel about that? Well, what was I going to say? They didn't miss by much.

— 7 —

When I first began umpiring, it was up to the home team's general manager to decide whether the game should be called off. But there were abuses. Some general managers would cheat. We were in Philadelphia, and the Phils were scheduled to play a Sunday day game against the Los Angeles Dodgers. I was part of Shag Crawford's crew.

The game was to be played at one, and Shag got a call at ten in the morning to say that the Philly GM had called off the game.

"They just called me and said the game was called off," Shag told me.

"Jesus Christ," I said. "It's barely raining outside."

"I know it," he said.

The reason they called it off, I'm sure, was that Sandy Koufax was supposed to pitch that day against them, and they didn't think they could beat him. The game was played at a later date as part of a doubleheader. It was typical of the shenanigans that happened when you gave that kind of power to the general managers.

As a result, the league gave the power to call off the games back to the umpires.

Years later, we were in St. Louis for a game between the Cardinals and the Chicago Cubs. They were playing an important three-game series. Before the first game, a scheduled two p.m. start, it was raining hard, and it kept raining hard all afternoon. I stayed at the ballpark, hoping the rain would let up.

I asked the head groundskeeper about the weather report, and he said to me, "It's going to rain all night."

By eight o'clock the infield was really muddy, and finally I called it. They were unable to reschedule the game, and as a result the Cardinals lost a pay date. The general manager was upset because it was going to cost him a lot of money.

When I returned to my hotel room, which overlooked the ballpark, I kept a diary. Every half hour I would write, *Still raining hard. Still raining.* And I sat there until one thirty in the morning, when I wrote *Game called properly.*

I then went to bed.

I sent my notes in to Chub Feeney with my report. Chub called to tell me he was taking away the right of calling the game and giving it back to the general managers. That was the dumbest thing in the world, but it was all part of what was turning into the corporatization of baseball.

I was watching the 2012 World Series on TV, and they called the game on account of rain. There was no way I wouldn't have started that game and gotten in seven innings.

My first trip into a town, I would always spend twenty minutes with the grounds crew. I'd visit with them, because I knew I might need them. And I could get them to do anything for me. They knew I liked to work in the rain.

I played the safety factor. If I saw somebody's foot slip just once, or my own foot, I would call time-out and order the infield covered. If the rain lightened up, I'd get the whole grounds crew out there and have them take off the tarp and put diamond dust all over the infield just like new. It would take them ten minutes.

One reason the grounds crew would do anything for me was that I'd bring a bottle of scotch to the head groundskeeper and have him deliver two cases of beer to the guys who were actually doing the work. They were the best. They were such hard workers.

When I retired, the New York Mets grounds crew gave me a Gore-Tex golf rain suit, acknowledging that I always worked in the rain.

— 8 —

If I had to pick one play that defines what it's like to be an umpire, that play occurred when we were in Philadelphia in 1979. The Pirates were trying to win the pennant. Chuck Tanner was the Pirate manager.

Keith Moreland came up for Philadelphia, the first time I ever saw the kid. The bases were stacked, and Moreland hit a line drive right down the left-field line like a 1-iron in golf. I was down on my knee behind the plate, and all I see was this big, huge back and the back of his uniform, number 22. I jerked up my head real quick to see where the ball had gone. All I saw was a flash of white down by the fence. I thought to myself, *Am I glad I've got a third-base umpire.*

I looked down at Eric Gregg, who was umpiring at third. I had always told him, “Eric, when you get a line shot, don’t ever go down on one knee. You destroy your line of sight and you can’t see a thing in the lights.” But there was Eric, all three hundred pounds of him, down on one knee.

Eric put up his hand and slowly went into this circular motion to signal a home run. It told me he wasn’t sure whether it was fair or foul. I’m sure it told everyone else in the park the same thing. On a ball like that, you gotta sell it. *Bam!* You nail it! You turn your index finger round and round. That’s the way you sell that thing.

When Eric stood up, he looked like he was being attacked by wasps or yellow jackets, because back in those days the Pirates had those awful yellow-and-black uniforms. The Pirates players swarmed him.

Chuck Tanner came running up to me. “Harvey, Harvey!”

“Get away, Chuck!” I said.

I had no idea where the ball was. All I had seen was that flash of the white of the ball. I couldn’t tell anything. I was just not sure what happened. So, shit . . .

I started walking toward third, trying to get Eric away from all those players. Both teams were charging us. Tim Foli said, “Harvey, Harvey, you gotta change that goddamned call!”

“Get the fuck away from me or you’re going!” I said to him.

Then came the big fella for the Pirates, Willie Stargell, and he was going crazy.

“Willie, I’m ashamed of you,” I said. He had that shocked

look on his face. "What makes you think I can't settle this thing? Get your people away from us."

Eric came up to me and he had a look of quiet desperation on his face.

"Chief, chief, you got that call?" he was yelling at me.

I just walked right past him. I went and talked to the other two umpires in our crew, Andy Olsen, who was at first, and whoever was my second-base umpire.

"Guys, did either of you see what happened to that ball?" I asked.

"Nah," said Andy. "All I saw was a flash. I don't know what happened."

"Well, you have to admit, it was really close, wasn't it?" I said.

And Eric said, "Oh, man, it was really close."

"Okay," I said, "that's good enough for me. That's a foul fuckin' ball."

So out came Philly manager Dallas Green, snorting, hollering, and screaming. He got real close to my face, and I said to him, "Okay, Dallas, that's close enough. I'm listening to you. What is it you've got to say? And don't blow out my fucking eardrums. I'm listening to you. What is it you've got to say?"

Now, if you've ever talked to people about me, they'll say they liked me because I'd listen. And so I listened to everyone, and then I called it a foul ball.

The shit hit the fan. I ran four of them that day. I think that was the only time I had a cross word with Mike Schmidt, one of my all-time favorite ballplayers. But everyone on the Phils was pissed at ol' Doug Harvey that day.

Pittsburgh won the game, and we went into the dressing room. Everybody was sitting by themselves.

"Hey, get me a beer," I told the clubhouse kid.

I sat down and started stripping my stuff off onto the floor, drinking my beer. My partners weren't too sure whether I was pissed at them too, because they didn't really help me out with that call. It was real quiet. Then there was a knock on the door.

"There's a lot of writers out there," Eric said.

"Well, just let them cool off for a while," I said.

"Eric," I said, "do you want to tell them what happened, or do you want me to tell them what happened?"

Eric wanted nothing to do with them, so I walked out there.

First I have to get them to calm down, I was thinking.

"Hi, fellas, what's up?" I said.

"Harv, we were wondering why you made that call."

"What call are you talking about?" I said.

"C'mon, Harv, you know, the ball you called a foul ball."

"It was a foul ball."

"Well, yeah . . . but, Harv, the ball just slid in there where the outer fence starts; there's just an arc about that big. And that's where that ball went."

"It was foul, wasn't it?"

"Yeah, but we wondered how you made that call."

"Gentlemen, that's my job. I'm supposed to see what happened and make the call. And that's what I did."

But I'd have to say, that's the closest I've ever come to being stumped.

— 9 —

After a while, I became known as an umpire who didn't toss many managers and players during the course of a season. There was a reason for this: My twenty-second rule had a lot to do with it. My stature had something to do with it, and my ability to make managers and players see the folly of their arguing also had something to do with it.

Montreal Expos manager Dick Williams, who was very intense, would really get into an argument. The game meant a lot to Dick. But Dick had a little bit of snake in him. He'd come at you really hard.

I don't know why managers think you're going to change what you called. I'm old-school. Al Barlick said, "If you call it, hang with it," and that's the way I umpired.

Dick would come out and say, "Harvey, what the fuck is going on here? For Christ's sake, can't you see that—"

"Just back up a step, Dick."

"All right. I'll back up. Is that better?"

"Yeah," I said. "But will you stop screaming?"

That's the way I handled it.

On the other hand, Al Barlick would say, "I don't give a fuck what you think." And he and the manager or player would stand there nose to nose until Barlick finally unloaded him.

— 10 —

As an umpire you are in charge, and anything that gets out of hand, you have to handle it. We had a rain situation in Chicago again, and Roger Craig, the manager of the San Francisco Giants, was upset because it had rained and I had allowed the game to continue. When it stopped raining, I could hear Roger hollering at me, so I went over to the Giants' dugout to see if everything was all right.

When I went over to him, I could see that their dugout was absolutely flooded up to the gunnels, right to the top, and I said, "I'm sure we can—"

Roger started screaming at me.

"There's no way we're playing in this fucking shit, and there's no way you can clean that out, and—" he was screaming.

They knew it was the last trip the Giants were making to Chicago, so they knew that ball game had to be made up in San Francisco, unless there was a day off around Chicago. And Roger started hollering at me because he wanted me to call the game, and I said, "Whoa, Rog, let me take a look at things."

I turned to the grounds crew and said, "Any of you guys want to make ten bucks?"

"I sure do, Harv," one of them said.

"Fine; you go down there," I said. "There has to be a drain that's plugged. Go down there and find out."

He jumped in as Roger started in on me again.

"Harv, I'm telling you. I'm not playing this goddamn game."

I let him holler.

The grounds-crew member dunked his head into the rainwater in the dugout, and he came up with a towel that had been covering the drain. As soon as he pulled it up, the water just gurgled out and disappeared.

I turned around to Roger and said, "Now, Roger, go inside, get your ball club, and get them out here. I'm giving you ten minutes."

"I'm not bringing my club out here," he said.

"You have ten minutes," I said, "and then I'm going to unload you and anybody that's around you. Now I'm going to go dry myself, and I'll be back out in ten minutes."

I came out, both ball clubs were there, and we finished the ball game.

I tried to teach my young umpires: You have to use your head instead of your mouth. Shut your mouth when they come at you. Don't let them get up close to you. Don't let them get face-to-face. Tell them, "Hold it. Hold it." They will stop. "I'm listening to you, but back up." That's the way I did it. And if you refused to back up, then I'd turn away from you and unload you.

— 11 —

One of the lessons my years of experience taught me was that you always give the manager a choice whether he's to be tossed or not.

We were in New York in 1987 and it was raining, and because it was the last trip to New York, I tried harder to get the games in. There was a very light rain falling. The St. Louis Cardinals' pitcher went out to warm up, and when his left foot landed, he slipped. Not big, just a little. He didn't go down, but whenever I saw that type of thing, I either repaired whatever was wrong with it or I covered the infield.

Whitey Herzog came running out. Whitey was hot-tempered.

"Jesus Christ, Harvey, you've got to call it off. It's raining."

"Whoa, whoa, Whitey. Hang on a minute," I said.

I called my grounds crew out and said, "Fellas, can you fix that spot where he's landing?"

"Sure."

The grounds-crew worker pulled a two-foot-by-three-foot piece of clay out of the ground, put new clay in, pounded it down, and covered it with Dry.

"There you go, Whitey," I said.

"Oh no, that's not good enough," he said.

"Son, let me see you throw the ball," I said, and the pitcher threw a ball and tried to slide his foot but couldn't.

"That's good enough, Whitey," I said.

"Like hell it is," said Whitey. "You're not playing this goddamn game under these circumstances."

"Whitey, we're going to play it," I said.

"Like fuck we are," he said. "I'm not moving."

"Whitey, you're either moving or you're gone. Now it's up to you."

I always put it in the manager's lap. If he wanted to be ejected, I just told him, "It's up to you." I always ended it that way. When he refused to go, I unloaded him.

"I'm not moving," he said after I tossed him.

"All right," I said. "Do you see that player sitting right next to your dugout? That player. I'm going to unload him if you don't leave."

"What do you mean? You can't do that," Whitey said.

"Not only that," I said, "I'll unload him and then unload the guy next to him." I was indicating one of the players in the game.

"Left to right, I will unload every one of them," I said. "Now you can leave or not leave."

Bingo.

"Aw, fuck it, Harvey," Whitey said, and he left.

That was typical. You leave it up to them. There's no sense for you to take all the heat. And you write in your report, *I told him, "Either you leave or I'm going to have to eject you."*

That way I'm covered. If the manager calls in and says, "Jesus Christ, Harvey is always ejecting me. How the hell can I—"

The man in charge of umpires then can say to the guy, "It says in Harvey's report that he told you if you didn't leave, he would have to eject you. Is that true?"

"Well, yeah."

"Well, then . . . why didn't you leave?"

"Well, I was pissed."

"So what do you want me to do?"

That was the end of it. He had no argument.

— 12 —

You're in charge, and that means you are in charge of the *whole* ballpark. That doesn't just mean on the field. You are in charge, and anything that gets out of hand, you have to handle it.

I was in Chicago, Wrigley Field, and the catcher for the Cardinals, Darrell Porter, had had to go through alcohol rehab. He hit a triple and slid into third. The stands aren't too far from third base at Wrigley Field, and two fans started in on him, hammering him about being "a drunken asshole, you fucking idiot." They were ripping him. These guys were sixty years old, and they were dressed to the nines. Each had a suit and tie on. I'm sure they had just come from work. I couldn't believe such trash could come from two gentlemen's mouths. They just ripped Porter up and down.

I walked toward them a little bit, put a finger up to my mouth, and said, "Gentlemen, *shhhh.*"

They started on me.

They said, “Fuck you too, Harvey, you cocksucker.”

I gave a nod to my usher friends—I’d made friends with all the ushers. I just walked back and as I watched, security came down, grabbed both of them, and jerked them out. I’ve ejected people from all sorts of situations. If I think they are wrong and acting wrong, there’s nothing in the rule book that says you have to take all that shit from anybody—and that includes the fans.

— 13 —

Sometimes a word to the wise is sufficient. I was behind the plate one day. About the fourth pitch I called a strike on one of the Dodger hitters, and the ballplayer stepped back to ask me a question. From the bench Tommy Lasorda hollered, “That ball’s low.”

I looked over to him and loudly said, “Lasorda, your pitchers can’t make a living if I don’t give that pitch.”

Tommy looked at me. He knew I meant it and he shut up.

I always had the feeling that if you had the proper answer, you could always get them off your back. It got to where during the last fifteen years of my career, I didn’t have any trouble.

— 14 —

One of my favorite stories occurred in 1990 when Lou Piniella was managing Cincinnati and took the Reds to the World Series, which they won. He had taken over the team, and they were going horseshit. Before the game, Lou knocked on the door of the umpires' dressing room.

"So who's that?" I asked Jerry Crawford.

"It's Lou Piniella," Jerry said.

"Tell him he has ten seconds. What's he want?"

I figured he wanted to argue about something that happened in the game the day before.

Lou came in and said, "Harvey, will you just do me a favor?"

"What's that?"

"I'll come out and start a little argument with you," he said. "Will you throw me out of the game?"

"You want us to throw you out of the game when you come out?" I asked with a certain skepticism.

"That's right," he said. "Because my ball club is going so horseshit that I can't wake them up. So maybe my getting thrown out of a game will wake them up."

That was fine. It didn't bother me. I didn't know whether that was considered a favor or not, but at least he came in and let us know what he was going to do instead of just coming out and screaming and calling us cocksuckers.

Lou came out in the first inning and ran to second base to argue a call.

Dutch Rennert, who's a card and a half, was a delight to have on your team, except that Dutch would just as soon get the game over with in a hurry and let's go sit at a bar and have a drink. He was great, sociable, and I just loved him and loved being around him.

Anyway, Lou went charging out and stood there gesticulating, talking to Rennert and looking back at me. He then turned around and went back to the dugout. Between innings he came out to me and said, "Harv, what the hell is going on? I thought you guys were going to jerk me out."

"Well, what happened?" I asked.

Said Lou: "I said, 'Okay, Dutch,' and Dutch just said, 'Okay by me,' and so I turned around and walked away."

In truth, I know what happened, why Dutch didn't run him. Dutch thought he'd have to write a report, and he didn't want to have to do it.

"I'll tell you what," I told Lou. "Move your arms up and down and act like you're pissed. I'm going to walk away, and you go kick dirt on my plate and I'll unload you."

"Okay," he said, and we did just that. He kicked some dirt on my plate, and I unloaded him.

After the game I said to Dutch, "How come you didn't unload him?"

"He didn't call me anything."

"Dutch," I said, "he wasn't going to call you anything. He just wanted to get unloaded."

"The game's not played that way," said Dutch.

"Okay, Dutch." And of course I wrote a report that Lou had wanted to jack up his ball club, that he had come in before the game and asked me to throw him out—so I threw him out. Lou didn't get fined.

Another time Lou came roaring out to second base to my umpire—Dutch again—and I walked out partway to be a witness.

"Harvey, don't come over here," Lou said. "It's his call. I want him to explain it to me." And he started in again.

"Lou," I said.

"I mean it, Harv," he said. "I don't want to talk to you."

What Lou wanted was for us to call the runner out for taking out the shortstop on a double play. He was arguing about the fact that the runner went after the shortstop, after he took the throw from the second baseman and went to throw to first base, and you can't do that. The runner must be able to reach the bag if he slides. But even though it was Lou's runner who went out of his way to impede the fielder, Lou was arguing it should have been a double play, because you're supposed to call the man out at first base if the runner makes an improper slide at second.

If Lou only would shut up, I thought, *I'll be able to straighten him out.*

"Lou, give me five seconds," I said.

"All right, Harvey, what is it?"

"Lou, what you're arguing about is a double play, right?"

"Yeah, that's right. A double play," he said. He was arguing, "You ought to call the guy out at first. If he interferes like that, goes out of the baseline—"

"That's *your man* that slid out there," I said. "You asked us to call a double play against *your* team."

Lou looked around, looked down at the ground, looked at his shoes, and didn't know what to do or say. Embarrassed (to say the least), he finally just walked off, because he realized he was asking us to call a double play against his own team.

Lou had the silliest look on his face. I always contended that umpiring for Lou was like umpiring for a high school kid.

— 15 —

During my years umpiring I got to watch some terrific managers at work. Among those wonderful managers were Davey Johnson, John McNamara, Bruce Bochy, and Jim Leyland.

Davey did as well with a good ball club as any manager I saw. With the New York Mets he had the horses, and he handled them well. He knew how to argue. He'd come at me, give me all sorts of hell, but when I told him it was over, he'd go back to the dugout and let us get on with the game.

McNamara, who led the Reds for several years, was one of the greatest people in baseball. I loved John. He'd ask a question, get an answer, and walk off.

Bochy has done the greatest job in the world, first in San Diego and then in San Francisco. Right now I think Bruce Bochy is the best manager in baseball. The Padres sold or traded so many key players out from under him, and he still put together a contending team. I think the world of the guy, and to watch him work was terrific. He was a guy who would come out and talk to you.

"Harvey, what the hell is going on out here? What happened?"

Jim Leyland was the same way.

I don't mind when a manager is a little upset, wanting to know what's happening. I can remember early in Leyland's career when he came into the league, he came out to second base four different times.

"You know, Jim," I said, "this is the fourth time you've been out to see me."

"Is that too many, Harv?" he asked.

"Don't you think it's a bit much, Jim?" I said. "I know what I'm doing."

"Okay."

And that was it. Leyland was a terrific guy.

— 16 —

One of the great joys I had as crew chief was training the young umpires who came under my wing. Two of my favorite were Jerry Crawford, Shag's son, who was with me for eleven years, and Joe West, a great professional and a dear friend. Jerry was a lot like his dad. I would talk to Jerry constantly about his temper. He would acknowledge that mine was the better way of umpiring, but it wasn't him.

I tried to protect Jerry from his temper, but it wasn't easy because he was feisty like his dad. He wouldn't take anyone's shit. If Gene Mauch went after him, he gave as good as he got.

We had a situation in San Francisco between Jerry and Giants third-base coach Dave Bristol that could have turned disastrous for Jerry.

John Montefusco was pitching for the Giants, and he was throwing a two-hitter and winning 1–0. The game was in the eighth inning and he had a 2–2 count. Jim Quick was the home-plate umpire. Jerry was at first base. I was at second.

The pitch came in to George Foster and he took a half swing. Quick signaled over to Jerry, who said, "No swing."

The Giants hollered.

The next pitch that Montefusco threw George hit nine miles for a home run to tie the game at 1–1.

The next hitter made an out, and as the Giants came off the

field, Montefusco hollered, "You suck," at Jerry—and *wham*, Jerry ran him.

The first guy off the bench was Bristol, who made a beeline for Jerry.

"What the hell did you run him for?" Bristol wanted to know.

"Get your butt over to third base," Jerry said.

"I asked you a question," screamed Bristol.

"I don't owe you an explanation for nothing," said Jerry. "You're not the manager of this team."

With that, Bristol took his cap off and in his anger whacked Jerry across the face with the knob of his hat. Jerry's head snapped back, because it really stung like hell.

Jerry balled his fists and was about to coldcock Bristol when I put my arms between his arms, held him back, and began to pull him backward.

"It's all right, kid," I said to him. "Calm down. Everything's all right. We got it. We got it."

I was talking to Jerry like he was an alligator. I saved his professional life that day. I guarantee you Jerry would have knocked Bristol's ass down. I turned Jerry away from Bristol and told him, "No, no, no."

We turned in a report to the league office, and Bristol was given a three-day suspension for striking an umpire. I thought the punishment was ridiculous. They could have struck a real blow for baseball if they had sat him down for the rest of the year. That's what Bristol deserved, and they didn't do that.

Baseball doesn't have enough control. The owners and the commissioner are too afraid of the players.

How can you command respect if a manager strikes an umpire and only gets a slap on the wrist?

— 17 —

Joe West, who was working on my crew, also found himself in a little hot water one day. Don Zimmer was coaching third base. Joe was umpiring at third. As the throw was coming in from the outfield, Joe whipped around to see the play at third. If the play is between you and the throw, or if the throw is off to the left, you go to the right. If the throw is off to the right, you go to the left.

Joe got down behind the third baseman, the fielder receiving the ball. Zimmer came over and bodily checked him. Well, Joe took Zim and threw him—and I mean *threw him*. Joe West was all-everything when he was in college. He was a quarterback, and he's strong as a bull. He whipped Don out of the way—I guess Don still has a plate in his head from a beaning a long time ago—and he said Joe tossed him right on the plate.

Joe made the call, and it went in Don's favor. But here was Don screaming and hollering.

We couldn't figure out what was going on.

I went running over, and Don said, "Get the fuck away from me." Oh, shit.

Joe and I—because I was his crew chief—had to go to the league office and explain what Joe was doing throwing a coach on his head.

"He was in my way," Joe said.

How can you make a call if a guy is standing right in your way? He threw him out of the way.

Joe was my guy. Joe and Jerry Crawford were special people. Shag, of course, and the guys who broke me in were in a class all their own.

— 18 —

I have more respect for Walter Alston than for any man I ever umpired for. Walter absolutely had common sense. One time he walked out and said, "Harv, this guy is balking."

"I hear what you're saying, Walter," I told him, "but what makes you think he's balking?"

"I'm watching him," he said.

"Walter," I said, "if I really thought I could see better from the dugout, I'd come and sit with you. But I'm watching him, and he's not balking."

"Keep an eye on him, Harv."

He turned and walked back to the dugout.

If that had been Leo Durocher, he'd have come out—"Jesus Christ, can't you tell a fucking balk when you see the fucking thing?" That was the difference.

— 19 —

One year I went through an entire season without tossing a single player or manager. I was afraid the league moguls would think I wasn't tough enough, so in the last week of the season I tossed Walter Alston toward the end of a game in which the Dodgers were getting blown out just to show the brass I wasn't a push-over.

The Dodgers were playing Montreal, and a little left-hander pitching for the Expos picked off three Dodgers at first base. Walter was upset about it. He kept coming out, wanting us to call a balk, and I kept telling him, "No, Walter. They're all right."

In the eighth inning Don Sutton of the Dodgers was on the mound. He jerked three different ways, and we called a balk. Walter came out to argue again.

The Dodgers were losing 8–2, and as he was walking back to the dugout, a lightbulb came on in my head. It was late in the season, and I hadn't had an ejection all year long. I said to Alston, "The problem with you, Walter, is you're a little balk crazy."

Walter turned around. We were standing near home plate. He kicked a little dirt on the plate, and I ejected him.

After the game I was getting into the elevator leaving the umpires' room, and I heard, "Hold it. Hold it." I looked up and it was Walter and his wife.

We rode up in the elevator together.

"Walter," I said, "I have to tell you. I set you up." And I told him the story of how I ejected him and why, that I had needed someone to eject to keep from getting criticized by the baseball executives.

Walter laughed.

"Hell," he said, "as bad as we're going, I thought maybe it was good for us, that maybe it would pump the guys up a little bit. But it didn't."

Walter understood. I always liked him. He was a terrific guy.

CHAPTER 15

THE COMMISSIONERS

— 1 —

When Marvin Miller took over as the head of the Major League Baseball Players Association, I knew he was going to be a success the minute he was hired. Before him, the guys who came in to run the union were fans who kept trying to keep the teams playing while they were negotiating with the owners.

Most people are fans. When a player goes to an outside arbitrator who rules on whether you're going to get a raise, nine out of ten times the ballplayer wins, because nine out of ten of the arbitrators are fans. They want to get to know these players. They want these players to leave tickets for them.

When Marvin Miller walked in, he wasn't a fan. He had been a tough-nosed head of the steelworkers union. He knew if he took the players and had them walk, baseball would be stuck with Triple-A players, and the fans wouldn't want that. He had them go on strike over and over again to get what he wanted for the players. And he won big concessions.

Bowie Kuhn, the commissioner when Marvin came into baseball, was—to put it mildly—overmatched. Bowie seemed uptight and unsure of what to do. I was umpiring the All-Star Game at Yankee Stadium, and in the middle of the game the lights dimmed. We stood around for five minutes. I was the first-base umpire, and I could see Bill Kunkel, the home-plate umpire, talking to Bowie in the stands. Finally I walked over there.

"Bill," I said, "what the hell is going on?"

"The lights are all dim," Bill said.

"Let me tell you something," I said. "There isn't a ballplayer in here who didn't come up from the minor leagues and play under these conditions. Why don't we ask both managers if we should continue? Ask them if they are willing to take the chance that the lights might come on when the other team is batting?"

Lasorda was one manager, and I can't remember the other.

"Hell yes," both agreed. "We're used to this. Let's go."

It was typical of Bowie. He was likely to have sat there all night waiting and wondering what to do.

(Bud Selig wasn't much better. Look what he did with one of the All-Star Games: He called the game a tie because the teams had run out of pitchers. He looked like a fool.)

Bowie didn't have much respect for the umpires. While he

was commissioner our salary was low, and we could feel that in the pecking order of Major League Baseball, we were at the very bottom.

— 2 —

After Bowie left in 1984, Peter Ueberroth took over as commissioner, and he was terrific. He would back the umpires all the way. I'm sorry the owners were able to get his job, because he had the right idea. If you threw someone out of the game, he'd hold a hearing and fine them, no matter what.

They got rid of him because he wanted to run baseball like a business, with him being the CEO and decision-maker, while the owners wanted to have their hands in it. As long as he was commissioner, things ran smoothly, but his having full control just didn't sit well with the owners.

After Ueberroth they picked Bart Giamatti to be the commissioner in 1988. Bart, who had been the president of Yale University, wasn't commissioner for a year. The thing he was best known for was kicking Pete Rose out of baseball and making him ineligible for the Hall of Fame.

It wasn't long after Bart suspended Pete that Giamatti had a massive heart attack and died.

— 3 —

When we were in New York, Bart never failed to come into our dressing room and see us, no matter what. One day he came in, all sweaty. He was in a hurry.

"Here, boss," I said. "Sit down."

I put him in a chair.

"Now tell me," I said, "what's bothering you?"

"I'll tell you something," he said. "I'm going upstairs for a meeting with all the general managers, and all they do is gripe about the fact that the old-time umpires were so much nicer than the group we have today. Tell me, Harv, is that true?"

"That's absurd," I said. "Let me count the ways."

"Go ahead."

I mentioned Jocko Conlan, Shag Crawford, Tony Venzon, and Al Barlick, the biggest of them all.

"I could go on," I said. "These are the ones who come to mind. If you as much as opened your mouth, you were gone. No doubt in my mind, they were far tougher than the umpires today."

"You're serious," Giamatti said.

"I'm dead serious. You go up there and ask the general managers what the hell they're thinking. Have they ever been around when Al Barlick started hollering? He shook the whole stadium, and he had no fear of anybody. If someone hollered from the bench, he'd turn and walk eight or ten steps toward the bench and turn that voice loose, and he'd bury them. He'd say, 'One more from you assholes, and you're gone.' That's the way Al talked."

Bart promised he'd go up there and tell them. I don't know if he ever did.

— 4 —

Fay Vincent, a close friend of Bart's, became the baseball commissioner in 1989, following Bart's death. Fay was the best. We could trust him. When he took the job he said, "The umpires are my police force. And I will back them."

I believe that Fay was kicked out by the owners because he cared too much about the players and the umpires. The owners wanted a commissioner who cared only about the owners, cared only about their bottom line, and so they picked one of their own: Bud Selig, who was the owner of the Milwaukee Brewers. Since Bud took over, we have seen a corporatization of the game. The owners came at the players with a demonic vengeance to reduce everyone's pay. The players went on strike in 1994, and the owners were so spiteful and stubborn that there was no World Series in 1994. They weren't used to being treated so disdainfully.

Under Bud, no longer are there National League umpires and

American League umpires. Now there are just umpires, and they aren't under the league presidents, but rather under the commissioner's rule. Umpires are now making more than $200,000 a year, but to get it they had to give up all their autonomy. We now have cameras in the ballparks to judge them. An umpire today spends every game with someone looking over his shoulder. Who can work that way?

The umpires went on strike in 1999. The argument was over getting more money for minor league umpires and for retired umpires. Just as the owners did with the players in 1994, they refused to budge. Richie Phillips, the lawyer for the umpires, decided the best thing would be for everyone to strike. Why not? It worked for the players. But they didn't realize how much Major League Baseball was being corporatized. Once Bud Selig took over, everything became about the money. It was no different from the guys who bought companies, fired all the workers, and then sold the company and made millions. There was a ruthlessness about it.

They ran into a buzz saw. Twenty-two umpires were let go, and about half of them never got their jobs back. The umpires today have given up all their autonomy out on the field. They have none.

CHAPTER 16

THE LAST HURRAH

I was in St. Louis and it was raining lightly. The surface of the field was Astroturf. I was umpiring at third base, and somebody hit a ball that I thought was going to be trouble for the outfielder, so I turned and started to head to the outfield.

I realized that the left fielder had played the batter short and wasn't going to have any problems getting to the ball, so I planted my left leg and spun on it to go back to the third-base bag, because there was a runner on second and I didn't want to take a chance leaving it open. When I spun on the Astroturf, my rubber-soled shoes caught—that was the danger of Astroturf. The shoes we wore had rubber nubs in them and they would catch on the Astroturf, and that's what blew out my knee. That left leg seemed to be my nemesis, and by the end of the 1992 season the pain took much of the joy I felt from the job. It was just too painful to continue.

The doctor said I'd be out of action for eight to ten weeks, but I couldn't stand not being out on the field, and I came back after five weeks. I had been taken off the 1992 All-Star Game because the league hadn't expected me to be back in time, but I called and told them to put me back on the game.

"Doug," I was told, "the doctor says you can't work that game."

"I don't give a goddamn what the doctor says," I said. "I'll be there."

I was stubborn. I shouldn't have tried to come back so soon. My leg pained me the rest of the 1992 season, and before the end of the year I announced my retirement.

For my final game after thirty-one years of umpiring in the major leagues, the league office called and said, "Both teams want you to work the plate."

"I worked the plate yesterday," I said.

"They would like you to work the plate for your last game," I was told.

I agreed.

The Astros were playing against the Dodgers, and neither team was going to the play-offs. I decided to have a little fun. Before the game I asked both teams what the game would mean.

"It'll mean about four hundred dollars per man," one of the managers said.

"Fuck," I said, "they spend that on tips in one night. Boys, ain't nothing on the line for either of you, so send them up swinging."

In front of the two managers I drew two lines, each one about six inches from the left and right sides of the plate. Bob Gibson would have been thrilled.

"Toes to the nose," I said. "That's what I'm going to call. And if I get one run, it's all over."

It was the fastest game that season, by far—one hour and forty-four minutes, and everyone, including me, caught his plane.

After the game, I came back out to the empty stadium to take one last look. I took my wad of chew and placed it right in the middle of home plate. Then I walked away.

I was done.

As much as I loved my job, nothing lasts forever. I had told my wife, Joy, I would quit when it no longer was fun, and in 1992, after I injured myself, it stopped being fun.

National League president Bill White called me in May the next season.

"Doug, I want you back."

"I'm already drawing my retirement," I said.

"I'll let you keep your retirement, and I'll give you your same salary, two hundred thousand dollars a year," White said.

"It takes too much out of me," I said. "I'm ten percent off on the strike zone."

"You don't have to umpire at home plate," White said. "You can even umpire at third base each game. The thing is, I want you on the field. I need you."

"You're kidding," I said.

"No," he said. "You run a better game than anybody. And I want you out there."

Bill wanted me there in case of trouble. It was said that I settled trouble better than anybody. But I believe a man's word is his bond, and I had promised Joy I would quit, so I turned him down.

"Once I quit," I told White, "I promised the wife it would be over with."

Do I regret having made that decision?

Only every day of my life.

A year later, I thought about it and realized I should have taken it. I'm not one to show off and do something just because it would have made me look good. It would have been different, something never done before. I'm not that type of person.

But I miss it. I miss it every day.

CHAPTER 17

MY MISSION IN LIFE

On August 27, 1997, my doctor looked down my throat and said, "Uh-oh, Doug, we have a problem. You have a knot about the size of your thumb that doesn't belong there."

They cut the thing off and took a biopsy, and a few days later he called back and said, "You have cancer—cancer of the throat. It's called Valecular cancer, the attachment of the tongue to the throat."

He added, "Take two months and get your affairs in order."

He was giving me a death sentence. I guess he didn't know me very well.

A month later, on September 24, our thirty-seventh wedding anniversary, they started treatment.

I couldn't imagine how such a thing could happen. I asked the doctor whether perhaps it was because I had played football or because I had been hit in the head and mask by foul balls when I was umpiring.

"It wasn't that," he said.

"Then what was it?" I wanted to know.

"It was the chewing tobacco," he said.

"Nothing else?" I asked.

"Nothing else," he said.

I wore another kind of mask when I went for the radiation. They strap you down to a bench so tightly you can't move a muscle. I couldn't have gotten up if I had tried. I wasn't in control.

I hated it.

For six and a half weeks they shot me with X-rays. I weighed 205 pounds when I started. I weighed 140 when they were finished with me.

When I speak to junior high school and high school kids—and I've spoken to hundreds of thousands of them since then—I tell them, "This is what you have to look forward to when you start using spit tobacco."

At first it didn't hurt. Then after a few weeks it started getting tender inside. I couldn't swallow food, so I stopped eating. I couldn't even get egg custard down. At one point I couldn't swallow a teaspoon of water.

I suffered from renal shutdown, which meant that my heart, kidneys, liver, and lungs were threatening to shut down.

They put a feeding tube into my stomach so I could have nutrition. Just as I was about to go home, I developed an infection. When I arrived home I was so uncomfortable I couldn't lie down on the bed. Every bone felt like a knife was sticking into me.

For four and a half months, I slept in an easy chair.

After I took my painkillers, I drank Ensure, which was poured down the feeding tube. I was warned never to cough. Try not coughing when you have to cough. One time I coughed so badly I expelled chocolate all the way up to the ceiling. Within twenty seconds my arm was burning. That's how strong stomach acid is.

Four and a half months later, my weight had risen to 170 pounds.

I was going to live. And when you have cancer, believe me, all you want to do is live.

I called Joe Garagiola, who runs an educational program about the dangers of chewing tobacco among ballplayers.

"I want to talk to the youth of America about this," I told him.

Joe sent me to dozens of junior high schools and high schools around the country to talk about the evils of chewing tobacco. In California alone, one out of every five high school ballplayers uses some form of chewing tobacco. Try it a few times, and I guarantee you: You will be hooked. It's made specifically to addict you.

If you want, you can look in just about any magazine for men or boys and you can find an ad in which you can order a free package of Red Man or Copenhagen or some other chewing-tobacco product. All you have to do is mark the little box that says *yes* and you have to mark that you are eighteen years of age, and it will be sent to you right away. Does anyone actually check to see whether you are eighteen? Not that I know of.

So then you try it out and right away, you feel great.

But the reason they want you to use it for free: After just one month, you will find that you are addicted. The lengths the tobacco companies will go to addict you are great. Ask yourself: Do the tobacco companies give a damn whether or not you get cancer, as I did?

When you begin chewing tobacco, pretty soon you notice that what you are using isn't strong enough, and you want something stronger. This is precisely what happened to me and to everyone else who starts out.

I started with Red Man, which is 1.8 percent nicotine, and I worked my way up until I was using Copenhagen, which is fully 28 percent nicotine. Once you begin using Copenhagen—unless you are unusually strong-willed and able to go through a painful withdrawal—you will need medical care to beat the habit. And sometimes even medical care isn't enough, because chewing tobacco is more addictive than alcohol, cocaine, or even heroin.

You want to save up a lot of money? If you're using a tobacco product of any kind, put aside the money you would spend on tobacco. I was spending $8 a week. That's $32 a month. By the time you turn around, you'll have thousands of dollars in the bank.

A lot of young baseball players think it's cool to chew tobacco while they're playing ball. Trust me, once you get cancer, you won't think it's so cool. I know.

CHAPTER 18

THE HALL OF FAME

— 1 —

I was inducted into the baseball Hall of Fame in 2010. After all the years of grudging respect from the players, managers, and the lords of baseball, to be treated with such reverence was almost overwhelming. I was treated as though I was a long-lost member of the family, the prodigal son returning home.

I get so emotional, it's still tough to talk about. And the bad thing, I had cancer and a couple of strokes before I went to Cooperstown for the induction ceremony. So in order for me to go from one station to another, to talk to a writer or have my picture taken by a photographer, or for a radio broadcaster to talk to me, ask me questions, and put me on the air, I need two people—one on each arm, helping me to walk.

It's thrilling now, because I can walk unaided. About a month ago I collapsed from pneumonia, and they thought it was over with. I called my two surviving sons and brought them in. One came in from Las Vegas. But now I'm feeling good again. Joy says I should have been dead about six times. So I'm hanging in there pretty good for an old guy who started out with twenty-two months in the hospital when I was four years old. I had to fight it then, and I've had to fight it all the way.

My trip to Cooperstown began with a telephone call. They tell you that you have to be at a certain telephone. You have to give them the number of that telephone. Then you have to be close enough to an airport to catch an airplane almost immediately. To do that, Joy and I drove from our home in Springville, California—gateway to Sequoia National Park—to San Diego, a five-and-a-half-hour drive. We took up residence with my son, got up in the morning, and had breakfast at a restaurant close to the airport, waiting for the call.

I hadn't been told a thing, whether I was in or out.

Why all the cloak-and-dagger? Because they're scared to death the news media will get ahold of it and break the news. They hold off until the last minute and then they tell you.

We were down in San Diego waiting for the call, and Joy answered the telephone.

"Doug, it's for you," she said.

I knew enough to know that they don't call you if you don't get in. I walked over and grabbed the phone, and a voice said,

"Mr. Harvey, you've been elected to the Hall of Fame. You're to be at the San Diego airport in an hour and a half."

I started crying like a baby. Hell, I get all teary-eyed now just thinking about it. I mean, I was awed. I thought to myself, *How could a kid from El Centro, who'd never been anywhere in his life, wind up in the Baseball Hall of Fame?*

Joy and I got on a plane and flew east to Indianapolis for a press conference.

— 2 —

I still had one more command performance in July 2010. The Hall flew Joy and me to Cooperstown. I had to fly to what seemed like the middle of nowhere, and they sent a limousine there and drove me to the Hall of Fame. I will say this: The ride was breathtaking.

I met the staff and was given a tour of the Hall that knocked my socks off. We were wined and dined, and the people were so gracious it brought tears to my eyes. Everything was first-class, just superb treatment, and the other Hall of Famers present were just so welcoming and gracious. All the old grudges disappeared, and instead we were able to laugh about them. Joy and I felt welcomed, and it wasn't always that way. They went out of their way to find accommodations for forty family members, in-laws, out-laws, cousins, nephews—they came from all over. It was such a great honor. There are so few umpires in the Hall. I was number nine.

I had umpired for thirty-one years. I made a lot of sacrifices, missed a lot of time with my kids and other family members. To have that induction was really wonderful.

The day of the ceremony was memorable. A few months before, I had been pretty sick. The doctors weren't sure my health would be good enough for me to give my speech in person, so I went ahead and taped one. Luckily for me, I recovered enough to make the trip to Cooperstown. I was on the stage while my prerecorded video was playing, and wouldn't you know it, it started to drizzle. My wife, who was wearing a beautiful purple dress and a purple hat, was getting soaked. I had to do something.

As a sort of joke, in my role as God, I put my two arms up to signal the rain to stop, and darned if it didn't stop within thirty seconds of my doing that. After the video ended, I told the crowd, "I want you to notice, I stopped the rain." They cheered and cheered. They loved it. So did I.

There's an old saying that they hire you to be the best, and they expect you to be even better. That's what umpiring is all about. It's a tough racket, believe me. I worked hard every day and never compromised my integrity, on the field or off. Being fair and honest is all I know. That's what got me into the Hall of Fame.

Ted Williams always said that hitting a baseball was the

toughest thing to do in sports. Hell, to me, calling balls and strikes in the big leagues is the toughest thing to do in sports. I'd have liked to have taken Ted back behind the plate during a ball game to show him what *tough* really is.

I've heard it said that umpires are a necessary evil. Well, we're necessary, but we're not evil. We're the backbone of the game, the game's judge, jury, and executioner. Without us, there's no game.

Before each game, no matter what, I'd tell my crew, "C'mon, boys, let's walk into hell."

That was my world. I loved what I did. It was my whole life. Just that and my wife and kids. I loved it.

By God, I loved every minute of it.

ACKNOWLEDGMENTS

Doug Harvey

I wish to thank my dad, who showed me umpiring, and my mom, who taught me a day's pay for a day's work. I am indebted to my brothers, Roy, Nolan, and Donnie, for always helping me, and I want to tell everyone else in my family, including my nieces and nephews, how much I love you all. I thank Fred Fleig, who not only gave me my opportunity to umpire in the big leagues but who did it when no one else believed in me. To Al Barlick: We fought for years, but you taught me. And to Shag Crawford: I thank you for being the man you were. I want to thank L.A. Dodger trainer Bill Buhler for keeping me in the game. I thank my friend Andy Strasberg, a baseball historian, as well as John B. B. Freeman and Richard Lister, for their hard work; my agent, Jeff Silberman, for his good work; Peter Golenbock, for his friendship as much as for his professionalism; and to editor Jeremie Ruby-Strauss at Simon & Schuster and copyeditor Richard Klin. You've all been great.

Peter Golenbock

I wish to thank my friends Ray Arsenault, Burton Hersh, Mike Rees, Ra Eisenhower, George Philippides, brother Robert, sister Wendy, and Genady Litvin and all his associates at Litvin & Torrens Associates in Miami. You all came through for me when I needed you most. I am deeply grateful.